INTR

C hristians are people who pray to God and speak with God, and some Christians claim to hear from God in the quiet of their prayers. Some even claim to hear from God like Moses of old, audibly. Some of our prayers are called *petitions*, so this kind of prayer is called "petitionary prayer." One Bible reader estimated there are over 600 "definite prayers" in the Bible![1] The prayers of petition are to be distinguished from prayers of thanksgiving and adoration and confession. Sometimes what we are saying to God doesn't fit any of these categories, or at least it slips from one to the other in a natural way.

Sometimes we are but musing, not even aware that we have entered somehow into praying. If one reads the Psalms carefully one has to think some of those prayers are musings, ponderings, and wanderings. Writers about Christian spirituality know from experience and conversations that prayer often takes place in our musings. On our walks or in our daily exercise or in our commute or over coffee or tea or staring out the window or in the dark of the night or upon waking a half hour or more before our wake-up time, if we think about it, we are musing. Even praying. Which leads me to suggest we pray far more than we may think.

To be in God's presence and then to ask God for something, or to make a petition as is the focus of this book, is one of life's greatest privileges and opportunities. But how does one petition God? *To You All Hearts Are Open*, the book in your hand or, as I now should say, before your eyes, explains petitionary prayer through what the Bible teaches and what the church has learned. The church has learned to form the distinctive form of prayer called "petition" into what is now called a "Collect." The Collect form for petitionary prayer, as a form honed from the Bible over millennia, instructs us how to petition God better. This applies to private prayer as well as public prayer.

Pastors praying, people praying

When I was a child our family participated in a Baptist church on the corner of Empire and Blackhawk in Freeport, Illinois. (Participated is a weak description; we were there every time the doors opened. We often opened them for the rest and closed them after the others had left.) Our pastor prayed every Sunday morning what was called the "Pastoral Prayer." This was his collection of petitions for our congregation based on what he knew of the needs of the church. Sometimes he prayed for fifteen minutes or more and we thought nothing of it. That's what pastors did. I don't recall my pastor's form of prayer, but I do remember *that* he prayed publicly. It is not an understatement to say *I learned to pray both privately and publicly by learning to pray like my pastor.* In my more than fifteen years of regular travel to preach in churches I can count on one hand—and not fill that hand up—the number of pastors who offer a pastoral prayer on Sunday morning. In addition to pastors no longer praying for the congregation every Sunday, the public prayers in our churches have lost contact with how the Bible models prayer and how the church has learned to pray its petitions.

We are in need of a revival of petitionary prayer, and I believe pastors can lead this revival of prayer. One reason we don't get our prayers answered is *that* we don't ask (to echo the Bible's own statement), and another is that we as a church have forgotten *how* to ask. This book is more about the *How* than the *That*.

I also grew up in a family where my father prayed at supper and also whenever we took a long road trip. At supper my father's words were often identical, but at times of personal fervor or when my father was especially moved, he prayed at length. I also learned how to pray by listening to my father. In some of my prayers to this day I sound like my father, and at other times like my pastor.

I also grew up in a church hearing life-shaping stories about prayer warriors. Most of these were about the elderly in our church who prayed all day long, or at least that's how it came across. I heard stories about John Wesley's mother, whether true or not now doesn't matter, praying

TO YOU ALL HEARTS ARE

OPEN

REVITALIZING THE
CHURCH'S PATTERN OF
ASKING GOD

SCOT MCKNIGHT

PARACLETE PRESS
BREWSTER, MASSACHUSETTS

FOR MY BISHOP,
Todd Hunter

2021 First Printing

To You All Hearts Are Open: Revitalizing the Church's Pattern of Asking God

ISBN 978-1-64060-616-6

    Library of Congress Cataloging-in-Publication Data
Names: McKnight, Scot, author.
Title: To you all hearts are open : revitalizing the church's pattern of
   asking God / Scot McKnight.
Description: Brewster, Massachusetts : Paraclete Press, 2021. | Summary:
   "McKnight seeks to rediscover a reliable path to relationship and true
   conversation with God"-- Provided by publisher.
Identifiers: LCCN 2020040057 (print) | LCCN 2020040058 (ebook) | ISBN
   9781640606166 | ISBN 9781640606173 (epub) | ISBN 9781640606180 (pdf)
Subjects: LCSH: Prayer--Christianity. | Spirituality--Catholic Church. |
   Spiritual life--Catholic life.
Classification: LCC BV210.3 .M385 2021 (print) | LCC BV210.3 (ebook) |
   DDC 248.4/82--dc23
LC record available at https://lccn.loc.gov/2020040057
LC ebook record available at https://lccn.loc.gov/2020040058

10 9 8 7 6 5 4 3 2 1

Published by Paraclete Press
Brewster, Massachusetts
www.paracletepress.com

Printed in the United States of America

CONTENTS

L ord of all power and might, the author and giver of all good things: Graft in our hearts the love of your Name; increase in us true religion; nourish us with all goodness; and bring forth in us the fruit of good works; through Jesus Christ our Lord, who lives and reigns with you and the Holy Spirit, one God, for ever and ever. *Amen.*

Collect for the 17th Week after Pentecost

one hour a week for each of her—count 'em—twenty-four children. More importantly, we had Prayer Meeting every Wednesday night at 7:00 p.m. where dozens gathered for prayer—first in the sanctuary and then in small groups. I not only learned to pray from my pastor and my father, but I also learned to pray and how to pray by imitating those I was hearing pray aloud. Hence, I learned to pray quite easily in "King James" English. So, "Thou art" was as natural as "You are." My father recently passed away at 90, and he prayed in King James English till he died, and now—I can hear him say—he is still praying that way because it's how he learned to pray.

Like my father, prayer warriors and weekly prayer meetings have mostly passed away these days. It makes me wonder how people are learning to pray today. (Other than having teenagers who drive them to learn how to pray.) Yes, by praying—of course. But what is their model? Their pattern? Their example? How do people in our churches learn how to ask God for what they want? How do they learn even to express what they want? Do they look carefully at the Bible's own prayers, including those outside the Psalms? Do they consult the many prayers the church has composed and then anthologized because they were so memorable and valuable?

I ask a question based on an example drawn from John Baillie, a pastor, a professor, and a pray-er whose book on prayer from 1936 has become a devotional classic.[2] My example comes with a lead-in question: Where did this man learn to pray like this?

> O GOD, ever blessed, who hast given me the night for
> rest and the day for labour and service, grant that the
> refreshing sleep of the night now past may be turned to
> Thy greater glory in the life of the day now before me. Let
> it breed no slothfulness within me, but rather send me to
> more diligent action and more willing obedience.

Well, of course, in church and at home. His father was a pastor. One brother was a missionary, the other a well-known theologian. He learned

to address God in King James English. He continued this prayer with
these petitions:

> Teach me, O God, so to use all the circumstances of my life
>   to-day that they may bring forth in me the fruits of holiness
>   rather than the fruits of sin.
> Let me use disappointment as material for patience:
> Let me use success as material for thankfulness:
> Let me use suspense as material for perseverance:
> Let me use danger as material for courage:
> Let me use reproach as material for longsuffering:
> Let me use praise as material for humility:
> Let me use pleasures as material for temperance:
> Let me use pains as material for endurance.

> O Lord Jesus Christ, who for the joy that was set before Thee
> didst endure the Cross, despising the shame, and art now set
> down at the right hand of the throne of God, let me consider
> Thee who didst endure such contradiction of sinners against
> Thyself, lest I be wearied and faint in my mind.

> *'But that toil shall make thee*
> *Some day all Mine own,—*
> *And the end of sorrow*
> *Shall be near My throne.'*

> Holy God, I would remember before Thee all my friends
> and those of my own household, especially . . . And . . .,
> beseeching Thee that in Thy great love Thou wouldst keep
> them also free from sin, controlling all their deeds this day in
> accordance with Thy most perfect will. Amen.

Indeed, the language, like an orange leisure suit, is in the style before last, the terms are artfully chosen, the expressions eloquent, but the desires expressed here are far closer to ours than sometimes our own prayers. Again, we ask, where does a person learn to pray like this? Yes, his father, his home, his church and . . . yes, his Church of Scotland. Yes, in the Bible, which gave rise to a history of prayer in the church, which formed parents and pastors and friends in prayer—and you and I today hear the accumulated wisdom of what the Bible generated. The first paragraph of his prayer above was generated by the form we now see in the Collects of the church.

We will begin then by looking at the Bible, where we will discover *the pattern for petitionary prayer*. The Bible instructs us by its own prayers on *how best to ask God for what we want*. Not all prayers in the Bible are alike, of course. But there are some abiding principles of prayer that can be easily gleaned by taking a swift pass through some of the Bible's prayers. In fact, the New Testament's prayers are rooted in the Old Testament, which is the pattern for biblical prayer, but the New Testament adds three important elements to the Old Testament's pattern, and we'll get to that in chapter two.

ONE

REDISCOVERING
THE BIBLE'S PATTERN
FOR PETITION

1

FROM THE PATRIARCHS TO THE KINGS

P eople pray and have always prayed. Like our inner musings and ponderings, prayer is natural. But we are not as praying a people as we once were, and one reason we don't pray (well) is that we don't know how to pray. One element of our not knowing how to pray is that we have somehow unlearned how the Bible describes prayers of petition. I base this lack of our knowledge on listening to people pray in churches and classrooms and in small groups. I am not trying to be critical so much as praying that rediscovering the Bible's own pattern for petitionary prayers might encourage us to pray more effectively.

To rediscover this pattern, we will look at some prayers in the Old Testament. Here are three prayers from the Patriarchs of Genesis,[3] and we can begin asking now what we might learn about prayer from these three early prayers in the Bible. We begin with Eliezer, servant of Abraham, sent on a mission by Abraham to find his son a wife.

> And he said, "O LORD, God of my master Abraham, please
> grant me success today and show steadfast love to my
> master Abraham. I am standing here by the spring of water,
> and the daughters of the townspeople are coming out to
> draw water. Let the girl to whom I shall say, 'Please offer
> your jar that I may drink,' and who shall say, 'Drink, and
> I will water your camels'—let her be the one whom you
> have appointed for your servant Isaac. By this I shall know
> that you have shown steadfast love to my master." (Genesis
> 24:12–14)

He addresses God as "LORD," which is the reverent English translation of the Hebrew name for God, Yahweh (or YHWH). He expands what he calls God by saying, "God of my master Abraham." Then he launches into a petition: "please grant me success." Which means "help me find my master's son a wife." He negotiates with God, asking that the girl who says specific words be the one appointed for Isaac. He *addresses* God and he *petitions* God, but his petition is also a form of negotiating.

Some people think negotiating with God is irreverent, and we might tell them to get over themselves. Abraham, the three men, and God, it might be remembered, negotiate about how many righteous people in a city would keep God from sacking it in Genesis 18:16–33. Jacob must have inherited the practice (28:18–22).[4] Abraham's negotiation with God over sparing Sodom is only rivalled in the Bible by Gideon's fleece (Judges 6). Hannah negotiated with God: if, she says to God, you give me a baby I will give my baby back to you (1 Samuel 1). Samuel, in 1 Samuel 8, seems to be negotiating with God over Israel having a human king (a monarch) instead of a divine king (theocracy). Hezekiah negotiated for more years to live (2 Kings 20:1–3).

Jacob

> And Jacob said, "O God of my father Abraham and God of
> my father Isaac, O LORD who said to me, 'Return to your
> country and to your kindred, and I will do you good,' I am
> not worthy of the least of all the steadfast love and all the
> faithfulness that you have shown to your servant, for with
> only my staff I crossed this Jordan; and now I have become
> two companies. Deliver me, please, from the hand of my
> brother, from the hand of Esau, for I am afraid of him; he
> may come and kill us all, the mothers with the children. Yet
> you have said, 'I will surely do you good, and make your
> offspring as the sand of the sea, which cannot be counted
> because of their number.'" (Genesis 32:9–12)

Here again, Jacob names God: "God of my father Abraham and . . . Isaac" and then uses "LORD." He then reminds God of what God had said to him ("Return to your country") and openly confesses his own unworthiness of God's abundant blessing ("I am not worthy"). He now comes to the point: "Deliver me, please" from his brother Esau, which is followed by a second reminder of God's promise ("Yet you have said"). He *addresses* God, he *reminds* God, and he *petitions* God. What is noticeable here is that he reminds God of God's ways as a way of petitioning God. This reminding is a form of affirming God as well.

One more: Jacob-now-called-Israel prays a blessing on the heads of the sons of Joseph (Ephraim and Manasseh), and this blessing is a kind of petitionary prayer that activates the blessing itself.

> But Israel stretched out his right hand and laid it on the head
> of Ephraim, who was the younger, and his left hand on the
> head of Manasseh, crossing his hands, for Manasseh was the
> firstborn. He blessed Joseph, and said,
>
> > "The God before whom my ancestors Abraham and Isaac
> > walked, the God who has been my shepherd all my life to
> > this day, the angel who has redeemed me from all harm,
> > bless the boys; and in them let my name be perpetuated, and
> > the name of my ancestors Abraham and Isaac; and let them
> > grow into a multitude on the earth." (Genesis 48:14–16)

Again, God is named with "The God before whom," "The God who has been my shepherd," and to this he adds words about God's angel ("the angel who has redeemed me from all harm"). Then he blesses the boys and requests that his "name be perpetuated" along with the name of his ancestors. He adds another petition: "let them grow into a multitude," which is one of the deepest promises and themes in the Old Testament. Blessing people, which is a kind of intercession and petition in which the praying person is invoking God to bless someone, has a high point in Numbers 6's gloriously beautiful words:

The LORD spoke to Moses, saying: Speak to Aaron and his
sons, saying, Thus you shall bless the Israelites: You shall
say to them,
> The LORD bless you and keep you;
> the LORD make his face to shine upon you, and be
> gracious to you;
> the LORD lift up his countenance upon you, and give
> you peace. (Numbers 6:22–26)

Some of the elements of the Bible's pattern for petitionary prayer have
now already emerged: addressing God, reminding God, petitioning God,
activating God's promises, and even negotiating with God.

Moses

The life of Moses is well known: born in Egypt, saved providentially
by the political leader's daughter, raised in the circles of privilege and
power, deeply cognizant of his own past, perpetrator of an act of violence,
a calling from God to liberate the children of Israel, mighty miracles
called the "plagues" followed by God's mighty redemption, the Passover
and the crossing of the Red Sea, the wanderings in the wilderness and the
giving of the Law from Mount Sinai, and heading north to enter in the
Land God has given to Israel. But Moses' dark side appeared once too
often, and God told him he would not himself lead the children of Israel
across the Jordan River. Moses made his grand, last petition, saying:

> At that time, too, I entreated the LORD, saying: "O Lord
> GOD, you have only begun to show your servant your
> greatness and your might; what god in heaven or on earth
> can perform deeds and mighty acts like yours! Let me cross
> over to see the good land beyond the Jordan, that good hill
> country and the Lebanon." (Deuteronomy 3:23–25)

He addresses God ("LORD" and "O Lord GOD") and reminds God of
his wonderful acts of power and deepens that with a huge compliment:

"what god in heaven or on earth can perform deeds and mighty acts like yours!" Only after these reminders does he ask of God what he wants: "Let me cross over to see the good land." *Addressing, reminding, petitioning.*

Another of Moses' prayers fills in this pattern, with the various elements of this petition in a different font style (this will be explained later):

> I prayed to the LORD and said, *"Lord GOD,* **do not destroy the people** who are your very own possession, whom you redeemed in your greatness, whom you brought out of Egypt with a mighty hand. **Remember your servants, Abraham, Isaac, and Jacob; pay no attention to the stubbornness of this people, their wickedness and their sin,** *otherwise the land from which you have brought us might say, 'Because the LORD was not able to bring them into the land that he promised them, and because he hated them, he has brought them out to let them die in the wilderness.'* For they are the people of your very own possession, whom you brought out by your great power and by your outstretched arm." (Deuteronomy 9:26–29)

Notice how abrupt this prayer is: after a quick address ("Lord GOD") Moses gets to the work of asking: "do not destroy" and "Remember" and "pay no attention." Woven into the fabric of these petitions are some potent reminders about who God is and what God has done and what God has promised. There is one additional element that fits often into the pattern for petitions in the Old Testament: an appeal to God to answer the petition with an expectation that God will preserve or establish his own glory, and this begins with "otherwise the land" and extends to "die in the wilderness" (bold italics above).

Addressing God, reminding God,[5] expecting God to establish God's glory, and petitioning or asking . . . these are elements in the Bible's own pattern, a pattern that has instructed and shaped the church's own prayers.

David and the Psalms

Close to the middle of the Bible is a collection of prayers called the Psalms, many of which are petitions that bring to the surface the pattern we are suggesting is at work in the way God's people learned to petition God. Here is a prototypical one, found in Psalm 3. David begins with the problem and his emotions and his experience: "O LORD, how many are my foes! Many are rising against me; many are saying to me, 'There is no help for you in God.' *Selah*." (No one knows for sure what this Hebrew term, *Selah*, means.) David is being taunted for his faithfulness to Israel's God. So he reminds God about God: "But you, O LORD, are a shield around me, my glory, and the one who lifts up my head." Then he tells us that God answers his petition: "I cry aloud to the LORD, and he answers me from his holy hill. *Selah*." Selah indeed. I have long appreciated David, king of Israel, spending line after line in his prayers complaining about his enemies. It has often made me wonder if politicians complain to God as David did.

Or take Psalm 10, again rich in experience and emotion: "Why, O LORD, do you stand far off? Why do you hide yourself in times of trouble?" That's pretty honest, and it is especially aggressive to open a prayer like that (Psalm 10:1). He then muses on the persecutions, schemes, boasting, pride, thoughts, curses, and many more things of sinners. All leading to this direct petition: "Rise up, O LORD; O God, lift up your hand; do not forget the oppressed" (v. 12), and then this harsh one: "Break the arm of the wicked and evildoers!" (v. 15). Why? He reminds God of God's own ways with "The LORD is king forever and ever" (v. 16) and this hope: "O LORD, you will hear the desire of the meek; you will strengthen their heart, you will incline your ear to do justice for the orphan and the oppressed, so that those from earth may strike terror no more" (vv. 17–18). David fits in the pattern: addressing God, reminding God about God's ways in the past, and asking God directly for something.

One of my favorite prayers is one that emerges from a powerful emotional experience that leads to nights of depressive musings and ponderings and then to rather sudden uplifting reflections on the ways of God. It is a psalm of Asaph and is found in Psalm 77. Most of the elements of the pattern are present or latent in this prayer. Prayer begins in human experience, emotion, and need for God. So Asaph starts in his experience, and he admits to God that he doesn't want comfort, and even thinking about God makes him groan in pain:

> I cry aloud to God,
>> aloud to God, that he may hear me.
> In the day of my trouble I seek the Lord;
>> in the night my hand is stretched out without wearying;
>> my soul refuses to be comforted.
> I think of God, and I moan;
>> I meditate, and my spirit faints. *Selah* (Psalm 77:1–3)

He blames God that he can't sleep when he continues with, "You keep my eyelids from closing," and he admits he can't even find words for his pain with, "I am so troubled that I cannot speak." As many of us do in the midst of pain, we remember the days when there was no pain. So Asaph prays to God and muses aloud to God if God might have rejected him forever.

> I consider the days of old,
>> and remember the years of long ago.
> I commune with my heart in the night;
>> I meditate and search my spirit:
> "Will the Lord spurn forever,
>> and never again be favorable?
> Has his steadfast love ceased forever?
>> Are his promises at an end for all time?
> Has God forgotten to be gracious?
>> Has he in anger shut up his compassion?" *Selah*
> And I say, "It is my grief
>> that the right hand of the Most High has changed."
> (Psalm 77:5–10)

A significant shift occurs in Asaph's musings at verse eleven when he
begins to focus on God and to remember what God has done in the past.
He begins, then, to remind God:

> I will call to mind the deeds of the LORD;
>> I will remember your wonders of old.
> I will meditate on all your work,
>> and muse on your mighty deeds.
> Your way, O God, is holy.
>> What god is so great as our God?
> You are the God who works wonders;
>> you have displayed your might among the peoples.
> With your strong arm you redeemed your people,
>> the descendants of Jacob and Joseph. *Selah*
>
> When the waters saw you, O God,
>> when the waters saw you, they were afraid;
>> the very deep trembled.
> The clouds poured out water;
>> the skies thundered;
>> your arrows flashed on every side.
> The crash of your thunder was in the whirlwind;
>> your lightnings lit up the world;
>> the earth trembled and shook.
> Your way was through the sea,
>> your path, through the mighty waters;
>> yet your footprints were unseen.
> You led your people like a flock
>> by the hand of Moses and Aaron.
> (Psalm 77:11–20)

The prayer, which is set up for a petition to liberate Asaph from his
pain, abruptly ends. So intense is his experience of God's ways in the
past, brought to the surface through musings and remembrances that

become reminders of God, that he has dropped his pain and his petition. The petition, however latent, is obvious: Deliver me!

Solomon

Perhaps the Old Testament's greatest prayer, if one were to play the game of grading or ranking them, is Solomon's prayer in 1 Kings 8 (this time from the NIV). I will use this prayer as an instructive example of the pattern for petition that has already begun to emerge in the Bible's own prayers. Solomon's request was for "the elders of Israel, all the heads of the tribes and the chiefs of the Israelite families" (1 Kings 8:1) to have the priests and Levites bring the ark of the LORD's covenant from Zion, the City of David, up to the temple mount—and this event was surrounded by countless sacrifices. Placing the ark in its sacred setting, the priests withdrew and "the cloud filled the temple of the LORD" as the presence of the "glory of the LORD" took up residence (8:10, 11).

Then King Solomon prayed, beginning with addressing God (italics) and reminding God (underline).

> Praise be to the LORD, *the God of Israel*, who with his own hand has fulfilled what he promised with his own mouth to my father David. (8:15)

> The LORD has kept the promise he made: I have succeeded David my father and now I sit on the throne of Israel, just as the LORD promised, and I have built the temple for the Name of the LORD, *the God of Israel*. I have provided a place there for the ark, in which is the covenant of the LORD that he made with our ancestors when he brought them out of Egypt. (8:20–21)

> *LORD, the God of Israel*, there is no God like you in heaven above or on earth below—you who keep your covenant of love with your servants who continue wholeheartedly in your way. You have kept your promise to your servant

David my father; with your mouth you have promised and
with your hand you have fulfilled it—as it is today.
(8:23–24)

The Petitions come next (in bold) and I only include the first few:

Now LORD, *the God of Israel*, **keep for your servant David
my father the promises you made to him** when you said,
"You shall never fail to have a successor to sit before me on
the throne of Israel, if only your descendants are careful in
all they do to walk before me faithfully as you have done."
And now, *God of Israel*, **let your word that you promised
your servant David my father come true.** (8:25–26)

**Yet give attention to your servant's prayer and his plea
for mercy,** LORD *my God.* **Hear the cry and the prayer
that your servant is praying in your presence this day.**

**May your eyes be open toward this temple night and
day, this place of which you said, "My Name shall be
there," so that you will hear the prayer your servant
prays toward this place.**

**Hear the supplication of your servant and of your people
Israel when they pray toward this place. Hear from
heaven, your dwelling place, and when you hear, forgive.**
(8:28–30)

The petition of Solomon comes to its near completion in words asking
God to be faithful so that God's glory may be preserved. The word "that"
in the second line brings to the surface another element in the pattern for
petitionary prayer: the desired goal of this prayer, its expectation if God
answers the petition (bold italics). Which itself flows into Solomon's
words to the people of Israel to be faithful.

And may these words of mine, which I have prayed before the LORD, be near to the LORD *our God* day and night, *that he may uphold the cause of his servant and the cause of his people Israel according to each day's need, so that all the peoples of the earth may know that the LORD is God and that there is no other.*

And may your hearts be fully committed to the LORD our God, to live by his decrees and obey his commands, as at this time. (8:59–61)

A long prayer, indeed, one that goes on for nearly forty verses plus six more in a kind of benediction, but one entirely appropriate theologically for the covenant renewal context.

Let's summarize now the elements of this pattern in the Bible's own prayers. The person praying:

1. Addresses God
2. Reminds God
3. Asks God
4. Expects God (to answer)

Yet, there is a lurking element coming to the surface in every petition in the Bible but mostly unexpressed: the praying person implicitly or explicitly expects or promises or hopes to be faithful to God and through that hopes that God will be glorified. This "Expect God (to answer) element" of the petition begins to appear in the Bible especially here in Solomon's prayer. (It will become prominent in the church's own prayer tradition.)

A question we have to ask now is, *What happened to this pattern when Jesus arrived?* The core of the pattern was already formed, but Jesus altered the Address, and the apostles formed a theology that changed how a petition was ended.

2

FROM JESUS TO THE CHURCH

We have isolated four elements in the pattern for petitionary prayer, but we are not done. The four are these: the person praying addresses God, reminds God, asks God, and then expects God to do something. We will soon see that the New Testament era changed this very little, but the changes that did occur made everything different. Before we turn to Jesus and the apostles, we need to pause to see that this pattern was common in Jewish prayers roughly contemporary with Jesus and the apostles.

Judaism

Israel learned to petition God in this pattern, so this is also the way Judaism after the Old Testament prayed. Here are two examples, the first from Joseph and Aseneth, an extra-biblical expansion of the account of the marriage between Joseph and Aseneth recorded in Genesis 41:45. In this wondrous tale of love and piety, with its beautiful prayer of blessing, the address is in italics, the reminder is underlined, and the petition is in boldface type.

> And Joseph saw her and he pitied her exceedingly, for
> Joseph was gentle and compassionate and feared the Lord.
> And he lifted up his right hand above her head and said:
>
> "*O Lord, the God of my father Israel, the Most High,
> the Mighty One,* who made alive all things, and called
> (them) from darkness into light, and from error into
> truth, and from death into life. **You yourself, O Lord,**

**bring to life and bless this virgin. And renew her by
your spirit, [and reshape her by your secret hand],
and quicken her with your life. And may she eat the
bread of [your] life. And may she drink the cup of
your blessing, she whom you chose before she was
born. And may she enter into your rest, which you
have prepared for your elect.**" (Joseph and Aseneth
8:9–11)[6]

In 9:2 his prayer is answered as she repents from idolatries; she
confesses in chapters 12 and 13; and the angel assures her of grace and a
marriage to Joseph in chapter 14. An observation that can be instructive
for all of us is this: notice how the Reminder is shaped to create the
petition itself. This will be discussed later in this book.

This pattern is found also in the most common prayer prayed by
observant Jews at the time of Jesus and the apostles, the *Ha-Tepillah*,
the opening petition of this prayer being only the address to God with
reminders of God's ways with God's people:

Blessed art *thou, Lord our God and God of our fathers, God
of Abraham, God of Isaac and God of Jacob, great, mighty
and fearful God, most high God,* who bestowest abundant
grace and createst all things and rememberest the promises of
grace to the fathers and bringest a Redeemer to their children's
children for thy Name's sake out of love. *O King,* who
bringest help and salvation and who art a shield. Blessed art
thou, *Lord, shield of Abraham.*

Here's a petition, and there are many of these in this standard prayer.

Bless this year for us, *Lord our God,* **and cause all its
produce to prosper; and bless the land; and satisfy us
with goodness; and bless our year as the good years**.
Blessed art thou, Lord, who blessest the years.[7]

This is the kind of prayer Jesus grew up hearing alongside his hearing of the Old Testament read and explained in synagogue. The pattern had taken hold in his world.

Jesus

I begin with the Lord's Prayer which, like many of the Bible's own prayers, is intentionally marked by brevity and directness. What we see with Jesus is the Address element in the pattern shifts: from God and Lord God and LORD the Address becomes distinctively *Father*. We note three elements of the petition in the Lord's Prayer: Address God (italics), Remind God (underline), and an expanded Ask God section (bold).

> *Our Father* <u>which art in heaven</u>,
>
> **Hallowed be thy name.**
> **Thy kingdom come.**
> **Thy will be done in earth, as *it is* in heaven.**
>
> **Give us this day our daily bread.**
> **And forgive us our debts**, as we forgive our debtors.
> **And lead us not into temptation,**
> **but deliver us from evil**:

In some manuscripts the Lord's Prayer had a benediction that intensifies the Remind God element and, while it is not original to the prayer of Jesus, most of us continue to use it in public and private prayer.

> <u>For thine is the kingdom, and the power, and the glory, for ever.</u> Amen. (Matthew 6:9–13)

Our focus here, however, is on the Address. Every prayer of Jesus in the Gospels, except one, begins with *Father*. Notice these:

At that time Jesus said, "I thank you, *Father*, Lord of heaven and earth, because you have hidden these things from the wise and the intelligent and have revealed them to infants; yes, *Father*, for such was your gracious will." (Matthew 11:25–26)

So they took away the stone. And Jesus looked upward and said, "*Father*, I thank you for having heard me. I knew that you always hear me, but I have said this for the sake of the crowd standing here, *so that they may believe that you sent me.*" (John 11:41–42)

"Now my soul is troubled. And what should I say—'*Father*, **save me from this hour**'? No, it is for this reason that I have come to this hour. *Father*, **glorify your name.**" (John 12:27–28)

After Jesus had spoken these words, he looked up to heaven and said, "*Father*, the hour has come; **glorify your Son so that the Son may glorify you**, since you have given him authority over all people, to give eternal life to all whom you have given him. . . . So now, *Father*, **glorify me in your own presence with the glory that I had in your presence before the world existed.**" . . . *Holy Father*, **protect them in your name.** . . . As you, *Father*, are in me and I am in you, **may they also be in us, *so that the world may believe you have sent me.*** . . . *Father*, **I desire that those also, whom you have given me, may be with me where I am, to see my glory.** . . . *Righteous Father*, the world does not know you, but I know you." (John 17:1–2, 5, 11, 21, 24, 25)

Then he withdrew from them about a stone's throw, knelt down, and prayed, "*Father*, if you are willing, **remove this cup from me**; yet, not my will but yours be done." (Luke 22:41–42)

Then Jesus said, "*Father*, **forgive them**; for they do not know what they are doing." (Luke 23:34)

Then Jesus, crying with a loud voice, said, "*Father*, into your hands I commend my spirit." Having said this, he breathed his last. (Luke 23:46)

The only prayer recorded of Jesus in the Gospels that does not begin with *Father* is the so-called "cry of dereliction," which says, "At three o'clock Jesus cried out with a loud voice, '*Eloi, Eloi, lema sabachthani?*' which means, '*My God, my God*, why have you forsaken me?'" (Mark 15:34).

This is a distinct contribution of Jesus and the apostles to the pattern of petitionary prayer. While not a law to be followed scrupulously, Christian prayer addresses God as Father.

The Apostles and the Early Church

We begin with the only two prayers recorded from the early church, and we see once again the pattern of petitionary prayer learned in the Old Testament at work:

Lord, <u>you know everyone's heart</u>. **Show us which one of these two you have chosen to take the place in this ministry and apostleship from which Judas turned aside to go to his own place.** (Acts 1:24–25)

When they heard it, they raised their voices together to God and said, "*Sovereign Lord*, <u>who made the heaven and the earth, the sea, and everything in them, it is you who said by the Holy Spirit through our ancestor David, your servant:</u>

'Why did the Gentiles rage,
    and the peoples imagine vain things?
The kings of the earth took their stand,
    and the rulers have gathered together
        against the Lord and against his Messiah.'

For in this city, in fact, both Herod and Pontius Pilate, with
the Gentiles and the peoples of Israel, gathered together
against your holy servant Jesus, whom you anointed, to do
whatever your hand and your plan had predestined to take
place. And now, *Lord*, **look at their threats, and grant
to your servants to speak your word with all boldness,
while you stretch out your hand to heal, and signs and
wonders are performed through the name of your holy
servant Jesus**." (Acts 4:24–30)

In this second prayer, "grant to your servants" corresponds to the
occasional element of Expectation. They are asking God to look at
the threats directed against them and give them power *so that* they
can declare the gospel. That second prayer continues, "When they had
prayed, the place in which they were gathered together was shaken; and
they were all filled with the Holy Spirit and spoke the word of God with
boldness" (v. 31).

These two prayers from the early church are carbon copies of the
Jewish pattern of petitionary prayer, though the content has changed.
These are prayers about the new redemptive realities in Christ. Notice,
too, that these prayers use the customary Jewish Address: *Lord* and
Sovereign Lord. Both of these prayers have a Remind God component,
with the second one quite extensive.

But there is a new theology on the block, and it re-forms the pattern of
petitionary prayer. There are two new elements, and we see illustrations
of each in Paul's letter to the Romans. In Romans Paul says, "I thank
God through Jesus Christ" (1:8), and in 16:27 he says "through Jesus
Christ" in a prayer, while in a later chapter he says, "you have received a

spirit [or Spirit] of adoption . . . [w]hen we cry 'Abba, Father!'" (8:15).
And some ten verses later he says,

> Likewise the Spirit helps us in our weakness; for we do
> not know how to pray as we ought, but that very Spirit
> intercedes with sighs too deep for words. And God, who
> searches the heart, knows what is the mind of the Spirit,
> because the Spirit intercedes for the saints according to the
> will of God. (Romans 8:26–27)

The two new elements added as it were to the pattern are about Access
to God, and the two elements are that Christian prayer is *through* Jesus
Christ and *in* the Holy Spirit. If we add these to what Jesus contributed,
we would say Christian prayer is *to* the Father, *through* Jesus Christ, and
in the Spirit. Our Access to God is Through Christ, In the Spirit. Here is
one prayer from Paul that exemplifies this very theology:

> For this reason I bow my knees before the *Father*, from
> whom every family in heaven and on earth takes its name.
> **I pray that**, according to the riches of his glory, **he may
> grant that you may be strengthened in your inner being
> with power through his Spirit, and that Christ may dwell
> in your hearts through faith, as you are being rooted and
> grounded in love. I pray that you may have the power
> to comprehend, with all the saints, what is the breadth
> and length and height and depth, and to know the love of
> Christ that surpasses knowledge,** *so that you may be filled
> with all the fullness of God*.
>
> Now to him who by the power at work within us is able
> to accomplish abundantly far more than all we can ask or
> imagine, to him be glory in the church and in Christ Jesus
> to all generations, forever and ever. Amen. (Ephesians
> 3:14–21)

God is addressed as Father. Paul reminds God (underlined words) and Paul asks God what he wants (bold). This is also one of the prayers in the Bible that ends as we end our prayers, with the Aramaic term "Amen" (which means "so be it," and so was said by those who heard and agreed with the prayer more than by the one who was saying the prayer).

Here, then, is the completed biblical pattern for petitionary prayer (and this is found in spades in the history of the church's prayers). The person praying (with the adjusted font styles that we often use below for these elements):

1. *Addresses God as Father*
2. <u>Reminds God</u>
3. **Asks God**
4. ***Expects God***
5. Accesses God Through Christ, In the Spirit.

I'm not given to acronyms, but if you are here it is: **A**ddress God as Father, **R**emind God, **A**sk God, **E**xpect God, **A**ccess God (Through Christ, In the Spirit). A-R-A-E-A (not very catchy, which is fine by me).

The appeal of this book is that we need not only to rediscover this pattern for petitionary prayer, but also to revitalize it. How can we do that? By learning how the church has adopted and adapted this pattern in its very distinctive petitionary prayer format called the "Collect." The Collect has mastered (and that's not an overstatement) the biblical pattern into an easy-to-use form that can help us in our own petitions.

TWO

RECALLING THE CHURCH'S PATTERN FOR PETITION

3

WHAT'S A COLLECT?

I f we want to learn how to petition God, the best place to learn is the Bible's own prayers and the church's tradition of petitioning God. To the point: we need to recall the church's pattern of petitions called the "Collects." The Collects (COL-lects in pronunciation) are the wisdom of the Psalms, the wisdom of the prayers of the Bible, the wisdom of the Lord's prayers, the wisdom of the apostles' prayers, the wisdom of the church's prayers . . . all formed into a succinct, direct, and theologically wise way of praying that both leads us into prayer and teaches us how to pray. A Collect is the formalizing of the Bible's own pattern of petitionary prayer.

In this and the next part of this book I will frequently use the Anglican *Book of Common Prayer*'s Collects, but this must be emphasized: *the church's Collects are found in all the major branches of the Christian Church* because these tidy prayers express the right thought for the right moment and have taken on special meaning over time. When the Reformation happened, there was what one scholar called a "stripping of the altars," an expression that describes removing anything and everything that looked Roman Catholic or unbiblical, which was (to be honest) a lot, including what was said and prayed and preached. However, *what was not removed by those in the reforming groups in the church was the Collects*. Lutherans, the Reformed (Presbyterians), Puritans, and Methodists retained many of the Collects, revising some and adding others. But they all knew godly wisdom when they heard it, and they heard it in the church's fund of Collects.

Take for an example the Collect for Purity, which is found in all the major branches of the church in some form. I have broken this wonderful prayer into the pattern's own elements, and once again I will code the words so each element can be seen:

Almighty God,

to you all hearts are open,
all desires known,
and from you no secrets are hid:

**Cleanse the thoughts of our hearts
by the inspiration of your Holy Spirit,**

*that we may perfectly love you,
and worthily magnify your holy Name*;

through Christ our Lord.

Amen.[8]

The church's prayers like this are not magical, but they are instructive because of their profound theology and wisdom of prayer. These prayers have the potential both to say what we want said and to say it in a manner that expresses it well, often better than we ourselves could say it. They have what Bridget Nichols describes with the terms "grace, dignity and restraint."[9] I would add: and "a long history, beginning with the Patriarchs of Israel."

So, what is a "Collect"? Here is a working definition of a Collect by L. E. H. Stephens-Hodge, an expert on the Collects:

> **collect**   A short prayer, characteristic of the western liturgi-
> cal tradition, that generally follows a pattern of (1) invoking
> God by reference to divine attributes or acts, (2) petitioning
> God for some benefit, often related to the invocation, and
> (3) pleading the merits or mediation of Christ. In the full
> form, a Trinitarian doxology follows.[10]

The term *Collect* comes from Latin and refers to collecting the people of God together to express their common petition.[11] One might say it is the "collected" petition of the gathered church. The distinction of Collects is that they are designed to express something a church would want, and their impact is that we learn to want what those Collects instruct us to want. They thus "collect" the various wants and wishes of the people and bring them into one crisp petition.

That brief definition above may be missed for all it says. In those three elements mentioned is an entire history of how to petition God, and those three elements flow directly from the Bible into the church's wonderful prayer practices.

The Biblical Wisdom of Written Prayers

Those who attend for the first time a Collect-using church are probably slowed down by a strain of Christians who are convinced no prayer other than extemporaneous and personal will do. Written prayers like the Collects, so their friends and family might say, are either "vain repetitions" or impersonal, and real prayers are spontaneous, extemporaneous, spiritual, and personal. And therefore, good and right and biblical. This worry about written prayers is not likely to go away anytime soon, so I offer a response.[12] The Bible itself reveals hundreds of written prayers. Then, too, Judaism's piety was shaped by written prayers, so Jesus himself learned Jewish prayers and then instructed his followers to recite the words of the Lord's Prayer.[13] The church has always written out its prayers. Written-out prayers, prayers prepared in advance, are very biblical. No one protested liturgy more than the Puritans, and the Puritans, too, wrote out some of their prayers.[14]

To fill this defense a little more, God gave us a prayer book in the heart of the Bible, and it's called the Psalms. These are not prayers prayed "one and done" but prayers that, because they were written out, became the prayers of Israel and were the prayers of Jesus and the apostles. The Psalms are often called the prayer book of Jesus, and the New Testament authors cite or allude to the Psalms more than a hundred times. No book is quoted in the New Testament more often than the Psalms, and the Psalms have remained the prayers of the church. I have heard over and over in my life that it is good for us to read a psalm every day and then pray that psalm as if it is our own. C. S. Lewis had a daily routine of walking around his rooms at Magdalen College praying aloud the Psalms in Coverdale's translation, and he attended a short service every morning at Magdalen College during which time a daily Collect was prayed. That habit of daily prayer led to his wonderful book on prayer called *Letters to Malcolm, Chiefly on Prayer*.[15] What he had to say about prayer flowed directly from the Psalms and the daily Collects.

The Bible not only gave Israel prayers to say but it also shaped their own personal spiritual disciplines. Observant Jews at the time of Jesus and the apostles turned first to their own Bible: they recited the Ten Commandments daily, recited the *Shema* more than once per day (morning, midday, and evening), and also formed a prayer they prayed at least once each day, a prayer called *Ha-Tepillah*, or "The Prayer."[16] The Ten Commandments are known by all, so I turn to the less familiar *Shema*, found in Deuteronomy 6, which reads:

> Hear, O Israel: The Lord is our God, the Lord alone. You
> shall love the Lord your God with all your heart, and with
> all your soul, and with all your might. Keep these words that
> I am commanding you today in your heart. Recite them to
> your children and talk about them when you are at home and
> when you are away, when you lie down and when you rise.
> Bind them as a sign on your hand, fix them as an emblem
> on your forehead, and write them on the doorposts of your
> house and on your gates. (6:4–9)

This reminded the ordinary Jew throughout the day (remember, it was recited several times each day) of the obligation to love God completely, and it became the "creed" of Judaism. In addition, as mentioned previously, a prayer that took on a function the way the Lord's Prayer does with many Christians today, namely, as the scaffolding that is used to generate personal prayers, is the *Ha-Tepillah*. I will provide here a traditional, King James-like translation of the first petition and then the ninth, a common petition.

Blessed art thou, Lord our God and God of our fathers,
God of Abraham, God of Isaac and God of Jacob, great,
mighty and fearful God, most high God, who bestowest
abundant grace and createst all things and rememberest the
Expectations of grace to the fathers and bringest a Redeemer
to their children's children for thy Name's sake out of love.
O King, who bringest help and salvation and who art a
shield. *Blessed art thou, Lord, shield of Abraham.*

Bless this year for us, Lord our God, and cause all its
produce to prosper; and bless the land; and satisfy us with
goodness; and bless our year as the good years. *Blessed art
thou, Lord, who blessest the years.*[17]

The beginning of this daily prayer reminds God about God and what
God has done before it turns to a petition, and the petition "Bless this
year" is as common a petition as one can find among humans. Common,
to be sure, but a daily need. These are once again illustrations of the
Bible's own pattern for petitionary prayers.

Now a third observation that supports using written prayers: Jesus
gave us a prayer we call the Lord's Prayer or the Our Father. In the
version less familiar, Luke's version in 11:1–4, the Lord's Prayer is
given to the apostles because Jesus was praying and Jesus' followers
knew that John the Baptist had given his followers a prayer to teach
them to pray, so they approached Jesus and said, "Lord, teach us to pray,
just as John taught his disciples." The "teach us to pray" in that world
would most likely have been done by giving a set prayer to use as that
group's identifying prayer. Jesus answers with nothing less than what
they requested. He says this, and this is my translation, "*Whenever* you
pray, say [or repeat this, or recite this]:

Father,
hallowed be your name.

Your kingdom come.

Give us each day our daily bread.

Forgive us our sins,

for we ourselves forgive everyone indebted to us.

And do not bring us to the time of trial."

Notice that Jesus said *whenever* you pray (and that means always). He was teaching his disciples always to pray this prayer. He gave his followers—you and me—a prayer to recite, to hang our prayers on, to launch us into prayer.

Finally, we need to consider the church tradition itself, because it recited written prayers from the very beginning. We find the Lord's Prayer not only in the Bible, in Luke and in Matthew, but also in an early Christian document called *The Didache*, where we learn of daily praying of the prayer. We see the practice of the Lord's Prayer all over the church throughout the entirety of the history of the church. Furthermore, the church very early on began to pray the Psalms as their prayer book and also to write out prayers of their own that were recited over and over in churches. Some of these ancient prayers are today found in the church's prayer tradition called the Collects.

The Psalms, the common prayers of Judaism recited in a daily rhythm, the Lord's Prayer, and the prayers of the church form a solid basis on which to focus this book on learning to pray with the church's Bible-shaped prayers. The petitionary prayers called Collects, stowed away as they were by our praying brothers and sisters in the Lord, are nothing more than an expression of this ancient, biblical approach to prayer. To deny use of written prayers, whether from the Psalms, the Lord's Prayer, or the church's prayer traditions, is to deny a biblical approach to prayer. Yes, by all means, we need to be spontaneous and extemporaneous and personal in our prayers, but the backbone of instruction is the Bible's own approach to prayer, and it includes written prayers. Enough said.

4

ELEMENTS OF THE COLLECT

We are instructed—indirectly but clearly—to pray simply and directly and clearly and boldly in the Collects. As Donald Gray put it, "the collect is content to say one thing, shortly and sharply, and have done with it."[18] "Say one thing" means "ask one thing," and in the Collects we petition God as we learn how to petition God. Long ago L.E.H. Stephens-Hodge outlined the now common understanding of the pattern of the Collects.[19] He listed the six elements of a Collect, and you will notice here a direct connection with the pattern of petitions we discovered in the Old Testament, which was then modified by Jesus and the early church.

1. Invocation: Addressing God
2. Acknowledgment: "who, whose, whom"
3. Petition: "Grant" or "Keep" are common terms
4. Aspiration: beginning with "that"
5. Plea: "through" (means)
6. Ascription: "who lives . . ."

These terms are not immediately useful to many today, so I have adjusted the terms—such as the term "Aspiration." When I talk about the Collects with students or friends and I use the term "Aspiration," nearly always someone ask what it means. I say something like this: The Aspiration is about the larger outcome, the expectation, the hope. Marion Hatchett, a major commentator on the prayer book, described this element of the Collect as the "result or consequence,"[20] while Alan Jacobs uses the terms "a hope or purpose for the prayer,"[21] but I have found that the term "Expect God" gives the most immediate clarity. Recall, I use Address God, Remind God, Ask God, Expect God, and Access God (Through Christ, In the Spirit) (A-R-A-E-A).

To give an example of how this biblical pattern shapes a Collect, take this much-loved Collect from the Sixth Sunday after Epiphany, and it would not be hard to spin the dial and randomly choose a Collect in any denomination's prayer book—or a book of prayers written by one person—to find the same pattern. I will order each element by the terms I will use in the book.

1. *Address God*: O God,
2. *Remind God*: the strength of all who put their trust in you:
3. *Ask God*: Mercifully accept our prayers; and because in our weakness we can do nothing good without you, give us the help of your grace . . .
4. *Expect God*: that in keeping your commandments we may please you both in will and deed;
5. *Access God Through Christ, In the Spirit*: through Jesus Christ our Lord, who lives and reigns with you and the Holy Spirit, one God, for ever and ever. *Amen.*

A second example is another well-known prayer called the Collect of Purity:

1. *Address God:* Almighty God,
2. *Remind God:* to you all hearts are open, all desires known, and from you no secrets are hid:
3. *Ask God:* Cleanse the thoughts of our hearts by the inspiration of your Holy Spirit,
4. *Expect God:* that we may perfectly love you, and worthily magnify your holy Name;
5. *Access God Through Christ, In the Spirit:* through Christ our Lord. Amen.[22]

Once one gets used to the pattern and sees the theological beauty to the pattern, one both likes and desires to pray like this and to hear prayers like this. There is a theological depth to this form of petitionary prayer that can revitalize our own prayers of petition, but it's not as simple as going down the list of the elements of a Collect.

Composing a Collect, however, Shifts the Order

Here is something we need to keep in mind as we learn to pray "Collect-ly." There is a three-part core to a Collect: Remind God, Ask God, and Expect God. They are mutually dependent on one another. When we compose a Collect, we begin with what we want and only then do we compose the other elements. If the desire of our heart is about an expectation we have ("that we might be more just" or "that racism might come to an end" or "that peace would rule in the world"), we begin with the Ask God element. Get what we want figured out first. The second element, what I call Remind God, is best known only *after we have determined the petition or the expectations*. The Collects then are not abstract theological truths about God applied (from 2 to 3) so much as petitions and expectations anchored in theology (from 3 and 4 to 2).

For some, it is best to turn the three-part core of the pattern of petition into questions, and to ask them in this order:

What do I/we want?

What about God makes what I/we want something God would want to answer?

What do we expect to occur if God answers our petition?

The fifth element of the Collect, Access God (Through Christ, In the Spirit), is not icing on the cake *but the sole basis for prayer.* We Address God, we Remind God, we Ask God, and we Expect God *only because of the merits of Jesus' death and resurrection and ongoing intercession for us*, as well as *the gift of the Holy Spirit leading our own prayers*. It is by God's grace in Christ that we are invited to pray.

A brief summary: we are recollecting how the church started with the Bible's own petitions and made them its own. We are recollecting the wisdom of the church about petitionary prayer.

Collects as Our Prayers

The Collect tradition in the church—this five-element petition—emerges with clarity and succinctness from the prayers we have quoted just now. What has attracted many to the Collects is their clarity and precision of expression to say what matters most in our desires, our fears, and our hopes. Yes, it must be admitted, there is a certain elegance and style to the Collects. Aidan Kavanagh knows this comes not by accident: "Thickening meaning," which is what precision accomplishes, "and then incrementing that meaning with style is no easy task, and it does not happen by accident."[23] The Collects have been honed and toned by centuries of petitioning God. The elements are not fashioned by some mathematician but by the people of God bringing their petitions to God—over and over, and in that over and over a settled pattern emerged.

Stephens-Hodge brings into full expression this attractiveness of the Collects—they are sharp and to the point, yes, but they say what we want to say and give us words to say what we are longing to say and, thus, after hearing them and saying them we say, "Yes, that's my prayer!"

> This perennial vitality of the ancient collects is due to the fact that they give expression to [our] basic needs and are couched in very simple terms. . . . [T]hey make their appeal to the hearts of [all of us] by their very directness and by their complete honesty. Here is no attempt to bluff God or buy his favour by specious pleas or multiplicity of words. There is no thought that we are to be "heard for our much speaking" (Matt. 6:7). The collects are more in keeping with the arrow prayers of Nehemiah (Neh. 2:4, 6:9, 13:14, 22, 31), with the cry of Peter on the lake, "Lord, save me"

(Matt. 14:30), and with the prayer of the penitent publican,
"God, be merciful to me, a sinner" (Luke 8:13).[24]

One can be instructed in the art of prayer by daily pondering the Collects.

Some Collects are designed not for Sunday worship but for personal or family devotions, and none is more succinct or beautiful than the Collect in the Morning; it is my favorite prayer of the Collects, and I mark the elements once again:[25]

> *Lord God, almighty and everlasting Father*, <u>you have</u>
> <u>brought us in safety to this new day</u>: **Preserve us with**
> **your mighty power**, *that we may not fall into sin, nor*
> *be overcome by adversity*; **and in all we do, direct us to**
> **the fulfilling of your hope**; through Jesus Christ our Lord.
> *Amen.*

I said this prayer daily, or nearly daily, for five years or more, and I still love to say it. And I have also said a similar Collect for the evening or bedtime, and it's my second favorite Collect:

> **Keep watch**, *dear Lord*, **with those who work, or watch,**
> **or weep this night, and give your angels charge over**
> **those who sleep. Tend the sick**, *Lord Christ*; **give rest to**
> **the weary, bless the dying, soothe the suffering, pity the**
> **afflicted, shield the joyous**; *and all for your love's sake.*
> *Amen.*

It should be said again that there are thousands of Collects, and each of the major traditions of the church shares them with the others. And, of course, each tradition has some of its own. Sometimes individuals have composed their own Collects. I have at times composed my own in writing, and far more often in my own prayers I mentally use the Collect's basic pattern.[26]

Composing a Collect on Restoration of a Relationship

Step #1: Write out the answer to "What do I/we want?" Ask God.

Step #2: Write out the answer to "What about God makes what I/we want something God would want to answer?" Remind God about God.

Step #3: Write out the answer to "What do we expect to occur if God answers our petition?" Ponder whether your petition leads to expectations of what you want to occur when God answers the prayer.

Step #4: Address God with the most appropriate Address to Steps 1–3.

Step #5: Finish your petition with the Access God element: Through Christ, In the Spirit.

So, here's an example of going through this order:

Ask God: Grant that We (use names if possible) may be reconciled through the graces of repentance and forgiveness into a loving, flourishing, restored relationship.

Remind God: Who is love, and who knows fractured relationships with his people, and who knows the grace and joys of repentance, forgiveness, reconciliation, and restoration.

OR better with YOU instead of WHO . . .

You are love, and you know fractured relationships with your people and the grace and joys of repentance, forgiveness, reconciliation, and restoration.

Expect God to answer: That we, who know again the joy
of restoration, and may commit ourselves to the path of
love.

Address God: Gracious Father,
Access God: Through Christ, In the Spirit: through Jesus
Christ our Lord, who lives and reigns with you and the
Holy Spirit, one God, for ever and ever. *Amen.*

Our Collect:

Gracious Father,

You are love, and you know fractured relationships with your people
and the grace and joys of repentance, forgiveness, reconciliation, and
restoration,

**Grant that We (use names if possible) may be reconciled through
the grace of repentance and forgiveness into a loving, flourishing
relationship;**

*That we, who then know again the joy of restoration,
may commit ourselves to the path of love.*

Through Jesus Christ our Lord,
who lives and reigns with you and the Holy Spirit,
one God,
for ever and ever.
Amen.

THREE

REVITALIZING
THE CHURCH'S PATTERN
FOR PETITION

5

ASSUME A PROPER POSTURE

Before we study the individual elements of the biblical pattern of petition, we need to pause to consider the very nature of what prayer is. Christians are people who speak to God. We believe we are heard by God, the Creator and Sustainer and Redeemer. We are being formed, through our Collects, into a people that genuinely believes and enacts petitions of a cosmic God.

At the heart of the biblical pattern is the expression of need. Miroslav Volf and Matthew Croasmun say, "prayer is an activity of those who haven't yet arrived and who aren't sufficient in themselves."[27] Amen. Remember one of the earliest prayers in the Bible, one from Jacob, said this (bold is for emphasis):

> And Jacob said, "O God of my father Abraham and God of
> my father Isaac, O LORD who said to me, 'Return to your
> country and to your kindred, and I will do you good,' **I am
> not worthy of the least of all the steadfast love and all
> the faithfulness that you have shown to your servant,
> for with only my staff I crossed this Jordan**; and now I
> have become two companies. Deliver me, please, from the
> hand of my brother, from the hand of Esau, for I am afraid
> of him; he may come and kill us all, the mothers with the
> children. Yet you have said, 'I will surely do you good, and
> make your offspring as the sand of the sea, which cannot be
> counted because of their number.'" (Genesis 32:9–12)

To ask is to be in a posture of neediness. To approach God is to come into the presence of God Almighty. To speak is to speak with reverence and humility. God indeed loves us and God is gracious, and we are not just lucky to be in God's presence. No, God welcomes us, but we are welcomed solely on the merits of Christ, so we approach God, not because we deserve it but because of God's grace. We come to God in a posture that embodies our relationship with God.

Humility

Humility has lost some of its attraction for those teaching ethics and virtues and civic behavior these days, and it seems to have evaporated from online public discourse, so we may need some reminders of how the biblical pattern works. The following petitionary prayer weaves in and out of petition, humility, and reminding God:

> May the power of God this day enable me,
> the nakedness of God disarm me,
> the beauty of God silence me,
> the justice of God give me voice,
> the integrity of God hold me,
> the desire of God move me,
> the fear of God expose me to the truth,
> the breath of God give me abundant life.[28]

If you read that prayer slowly, all resources are turned from us to God and all our power comes from God. It's a healthy reminder of the proper posture for all prayer, especially petitionary prayer.

Another prayer that emphasizes humility and, in addition, is also literarily beautiful is the church-wide Prayer of Humble Access.[29] It is often said by a minister of the gospel after breaking the bread and before the bread and wine are given to the worshipers. It is obviously quite instructive, reminding those in attendance of the need for reverence, humility, and confession.

We do not presume to come to this thy Table, *O merciful Lord*, trusting in our own righteousness, but in thy manifold and great mercies. We are not worthy so much as to gather up the crumbs under thy Table. <u>But thou art the same Lord whose property is always to have mercy</u>.

Grant us therefore, gracious Lord, so to eat the flesh of thy dear Son Jesus Christ, and to drink his blood, *that we may evermore dwell in him, and he in us. Amen.*[30]

To remind us of the avoidance of themes of humility in modern culture and worship, we observe that this prayer's rather strong emphasis on our unworthiness has met our modern and post-modern self-esteem movement and been relegated in Anglican worship to Holy Eucharist Rite I, which is the traditional wording not used so often. In its place in Rite II, which is more contemporary, we move straight to these words:

The Gifts of God for the People of God. Take them in remembrance that Christ died for you, and feed on him in your hearts by faith, with thanksgiving.[31]

The petitions in the Collects (and prayers) in the *Book of Common Prayer* are through and through expressions of asking for God to act in grace to us, so the old Prayer of Humble Access is organic to Anglican worship and deserves to be restored to its proper place. It deserves to be restored at least occasionally because we need to be reminded of our unworthiness and our need for humility in coming to the Table.

The church, when globally considered in its liturgical churches, has no small emphasis on the posture of humility in our prayers and petitions.

Seasons of the Church Calendar

Now for a little exploration of how the Collects of the church calendar, which again are found in all historic denominations, value humility, preparation, confession, and forgiveness. Advent is not about "Joy to the

World" and Christmas music like "We Wish You a Merry Christmas," but about preparation for the coming of Christ, so it sets the tone for the church year and it prepares us for the redemption to come. Not surprisingly, the petitions of Lent ask God for the grace of contrition so the petitioner rediscovers forgiveness, the grace of repentance and faith and faithfulness, as well as a love and desire for the good things of God. So the petition for Ash Wednesday is noticeably about contrite hearts being formed in us by God's grace. Ash Wednesday leads onward to Holy Week and God's great act of redemption in Christ. In the liturgical traditions the petitions from Advent through Lent, then, frequently express or assume the need for humility.

The Two Terms of our Petitions: Grant and Keep

The petitions of the entire church's prayer tradition are shaped by two terms: Grant and Keep. If one tallies all the Collects in *The Book of Common Prayer* (and we are focusing only on those used on Sundays) there are forty-three "grants" and eleven "keeps." The term "grant" petitions God to give us something, while "keep" petitions God to preserve and protect us in the way of faithfulness. The one who uses the terms "grant" and "keep" needs something he or she can't do. It is the case that for some the words can become little more than something to say before the public reading of Scripture. But if one "collects" oneself, pausing in the quietness of the heart to read the words first and only then to say them aloud in private prayer, humility is given the opportunity to take root. To prepare ourselves for the redemption in Christ and to confess our sins as we do in Advent and Lent, or to ask God what is expressed in one of the most memorable church prayers: "grant your people grace to love what you command and desire what you promise" (Fifth Sunday of Lent) is to admit that we need God's grace.

Similarly, to pray "keep" is to admit publicly and personally that we cannot be faithful without God's grace of preservation. On the Third Sunday in Lent many pray, "Keep us both outwardly in our bodies and inwardly in our souls, that we may be defended from all adversities which may happen to the body, and from all evil thoughts which may assault and hurt the soul." If holiness and obedience are the tone of that "keep," another one is about theological faithfulness: "Keep us steadfast in this faith and worship, and bring us at last to see you in your one and eternal glory, O Father" (Trinity Sunday).

We may think we have come a long way from Jacob's "I am not worthy," but not really: his humility has woven itself into the inner fabric of the church's wisdom on petitionary prayer. To ask God is to be formed into the posture of humility. In such a posture we now turn to the biblical and church elements of the pattern for petitions, beginning where we all need to begin: with what we want and what we desire, and what prompts our turning to God to petition our great and merciful God.

Now we turn to discussions of each of the five elements in the pattern of petitions that grow up in the Bible and are trimmed into order in the universal church's Collects.

6

ASK GOD

When we pray, we are not to barge in with "Gimme gimme gimme!" Instead, we begin with the address and often with some reminders about God before we articulate what we want. But that "want" is what gives rise to everything else in the petition. So, we begin with the question, What do I/we want? The prayers of the Bible and the church instruct us on the content of our petitions.

When I was about five years old my wealthy aunt took me to a big store in St. Louis and told me I could have anything I wanted. I asked for a first baseman's glove. I had never played that position ever that I recall, but we were going to a St. Louis Cardinals game and I was going to be ready. (My parents considered my choice of a baseball glove a wasted opportunity to get something valuable.) If we asked a teenager today what they would ask for if they could have anything they wanted, what would they ask for? What if we asked a twentysomething? A fiftysomething? What about a ninetysomething? Here's what Lydia Sohn, in her interviewing of ninetysomethings, discovered that they most regretted. In expressing their regrets, these were their top five they wish they could now reverse:[32]

> They regretted not cultivating closer relationships with their children.
> They regretted not putting their children on the right path in life.
> They regretted not taking risks to be more loving, such as being more open about their feelings for new people or more affectionate with those already in their lives.

They regretted not being better listeners; they wish they had
been more empathetic and considerate.
They regretted not spending enough time with the people
they loved.

We can flip these into what they would have wanted if they could do
it all over again and, thus, what they could have prayed for in those days.
The wisdom of these ninetysomethings is a wisdom that could inform
our prayers today. Who would we most want to be with us in our dying
days? Perhaps we should pray now for the kind of relationship with those
persons now.

If our exploration of the biblical and church pattern for petitions
teaches us anything, it teaches us to *ask God for what we really want.*
Like this beautiful Celtic prayer that is filled with petitions for God to
be with us throughout the day, each also a reminder of what about God
makes each petition reasonable:

> Christ, as a light
> Illumine and guide me.
> Christ, as a shield
> Overshadow me.
> Christ under me;
> Christ over me;
> Christ beside me
> On my left and my right.
> This day be within and without me,
> Lowly and meek, yet all-powerful.
> Be in the heart of each to whom I speak;
> In the mouth of each who speaks unto me.
> This day be within and without me,
> Lowly and meek, yet all-powerful.
> Christ as a light;
> Christ as a shield;
> Christ beside me
> On my left and my right.[33]

We turn now to a sampling of the content of various prayers of petition. The things we Ask God for are as numerous as there are humans in prayer! I will mention eight.

Ask God for Mercy

The central theme of the gospel is "Christ as Lord and Savior." Redemption then is at the core of the Christian faith, and that means asking God for mercy. Here I want to provide something we pray together every week at the Church of the Redeemer, namely, the prayer of confession prior to Eucharist:

> Most merciful God,
>
> We confess that we have sinned against you in thought,
> word, and deed,
> By what we have done, and by what we have left undone.
>
> We have not loved you with our whole heart; we have not
> loved our neighbors as ourselves.
>
> We are truly sorry and we humbly repent.
>
> For the sake of your Son Jesus Christ, **have mercy on us
> and forgive us;**
> That we may delight in your will, and walk in your ways, to
> the glory of your Name. Amen.[34]

John R. W. Stott, one of the last generation's leading evangelical pastors, theologians, and evangelists, articulates in three petitions what it means to ask God for mercy:

> Lord Jesus Christ, we humbly thank thee that thou didst
> choose bread and wine to be the emblems of thy sacred
> Body and Blood, given on the cross for the sins of the

world, and didst command us thus to remember thee.

Deepen our repentance,

Strengthen our faith,

And increase our love for the brethren,

That, eating and drinking the sacrament of our redemption,
we may truly feed on thee in our hearts with thanksgiving,
for the sake of thy great and worthy name.[35]

Ask God for Christoformity

Not only do we ask God for mercy, but we also ask God to reshape us
into Christlikeness, or what I prefer to call "Christoformity."

The apostle Paul prayed that the Ephesians would participate in
Christ and that through the Spirit would become like Christ. Here are his
words, and I place again in bold his doubled petition for Christlikeness:

> For this reason I bow my knees before the *Father*, from
> whom every family in heaven and on earth takes its name.
> **I pray that, according to the riches of his glory, he may**
> **grant that you may be strengthened in your inner being**
> **with power through his Spirit, and that Christ may dwell**
> **in your hearts through faith, as you are being rooted and**
> **grounded in love.**
> **I pray that you may have the power to comprehend, with**
> **all the saints, what is the breadth and length and height**
> **and depth, and to know the love of Christ that surpasses**
> **knowledge, so that you may be filled with all the fullness**
> **of God** [who is Christ!]. (Ephesians 3:14–19)

The Second Sunday after Christmas has a beautiful prayer in the
Anglican *Book of Common Prayer* about our union with and participation
in Christ, instructing us that our Christoformity is nothing but the result
of God working in us through the Spirit as a result of our union with
Christ:

O God, who wonderfully created, and yet more wonderfully
restored, the dignity of human nature: *Grant that we may
share the divine life of him who humbled himself to share
our humanity*, your Son Jesus Christ; who lives and reigns
with you, in the unity of the Holy Spirit, one God, for ever
and ever. Amen.

Here are three more beautiful instances of petitioning God for
Christoformity. On the Last Sunday after the Epiphany, just before Ash
Wednesday, Christoformity becomes cruciform: "O God, who before
the passion of your only-begotten Son revealed his glory upon the
holy mountain: Grant to us that we, beholding by faith the light of his
countenance, may be strengthened to bear our cross, and be changed into
his likeness from glory to glory." On Palm Sunday, or the Sunday of the
Passion, we anticipate the entire week in these words: "Almighty and
everliving God, in your tender love for the human race you sent your Son
our Savior Jesus Christ to take upon him our nature, and to suffer death
upon the cross, giving us the example of his great humility: Mercifully
grant that we may walk in the way of his suffering, and also share in
his resurrection." No day is higher in our worship than Easter, but on
that day we pray a Collect for nothing less than radical Christoformity:
"Grant us so to die daily to sin, that we may evermore live with him in
the joy of his resurrection."

Others echo these Christoform prayer requests, and this is one of my
favorites:

> Jesus our brother,
> you followed the necessary path
> and were broken on our behalf.
> May we neither cling to our pain
> nor refuse to embrace the cost
> when it is required of us:
> that in losing our selves for your sake
> we may be brought to new life. **Amen**.[36]

Ask God for Ordinary Blessings in Life

We move to another theme in the church's petitions.

Most people who pray petition God about ordinary events in life, at least "ordinary" to others but which are highly important in one's own life. I remember praying hard when our daughter, Laura, was on the market for her first teaching opportunity and then when she applied to her present school in the Chicago suburbs. I remember, too, praying hard for our son, Lukas, when he was playing minor league baseball and when he discovered his own career in the front office for the Chicago Cubs. "Our Father, you want each of us to find and flourish in what you designed us to be and do; grant . . ."

So, when we read Naomi's prayers for her Moabite daughters-in-law, both of whom who have lost their husbands, we are not one bit surprised that these sorts of concerns emerge in the prayer lives of God's people. Naomi has lost her own husband (Elimelek—"My God is king"), and they have lost theirs, so she decides to return to Judah. She says, on the verge of leaving her daughters:

> But Naomi said to her two daughters-in-law, "Go back each
> of you to your mother's house. **May the Lord deal kindly**
> **with you, as you have dealt with the dead and with me.**
> **The Lord grant that you may find security, each of you**
> **in the house of your husband**." Then she kissed them, and
> they wept aloud. They said to her, "No, we will return with
> you to your people." (Ruth 1:8–10)

One chooses to stay in Moab (Orpah), the other (Ruth) clings to Naomi. Ruth expresses her own commitment to Naomi as well as her petition to God with these words:

> But Ruth said,
>
> "Do not press me to leave you
>   or to turn back from following you!

Where you go, I will go;
   Where you lodge, I will lodge;
your people shall be my people,
   and your God my God.
Where you die, I will die—
   there will I be buried.
May the LORD do thus and so to me,
   and more as well,
if even death parts me from you!" (1:16–17)

Ordinary, indeed. Asking God in the ordinary occurs yet again in Ruth when Naomi, seeking a good place to land for Ruth, realizes Ruth had spent the day laboring in Boaz's fields. Her prayer request, nothing if not an understatement of her hope for Ruth to find her way into his home, comes out like this: "May he [Boaz] be blessed by Yahweh, who hasn't abandoned his commitment with the living and the dead" (2:20, *The First Testament*).[37] This is a prayer for God to awaken the man to her daughter-in-law. Indeed, the story opens up to Ruth making herself available to Boaz and Boaz recognizing that he can be her "restorer" back to a good station in life. After engaging the man who legally precedes Boaz in restoring the woman, Boaz is legally permitted to marry Ruth, which he does. The court of men making that decision then offer their own petition for Boaz and Ruth: "Witnesses! **May Yahweh make the woman who is coming into your house**" (4:11, *The First Testament*)[38] fertile! And indeed she is! What many of us learn over time is what Ruth and Naomi learned: what seemed ordinary at the moment, however emotionally significant, turned out to be colossal in life's importance. Ruth was to become the great-grandmother of David the king.

David becoming king makes Ruth and Naomi and Boaz a wondrous story, but let's not forget to see this all from other angles: For Naomi—who wanted so badly for her faithful daughter-in-law to have a husband and a new life; for Ruth—who though a foreigner, an immigrant, and one outside the covenant, wanted to have a husband who could restore her to society; and Boaz—who followed the law in his desire to marry this young Moabitess. All very ordinary desires, all very ordinary prayer requests.

Ask God for Healing

David was not afraid to ask God to heal his son: "David therefore pleaded with God for the child; David fasted, and went in and lay all night on the ground" (2 Samuel 12:16). Jesus was unafraid to ask for healing, and we overhear him speaking the language he learned at home, Aramaic:

> They brought to him a deaf man who had an impediment in his speech; and they begged him to lay his hand on him. He took him aside in private, away from the crowd, and put his fingers into his ears, and he spat and touched his tongue. Then looking up to heaven, he sighed and said to him, "**Ephphatha**," that is, "**Be opened**." And immediately his ears were opened, his tongue was released, and he spoke plainly. (Mark 7:32–35)

Peter prayed in the name of Jesus for a crippled beggar to be healed:

> And a man lame from birth was being carried in. People would lay him daily at the gate of the temple called the Beautiful Gate so that he could ask for alms from those entering the temple. When he saw Peter and John about to go into the temple, he asked them for alms. Peter looked intently at him, as did John, and said, "Look at us." And he fixed his attention on them, expecting to receive something from them. But Peter said, "I have no silver or gold, but what I have I give you; in the name of Jesus Christ of Nazareth, **stand up and walk**." And he took him by the right hand and raised him up; and immediately his feet and ankles were made strong. Jumping up, he stood and began to walk, and he entered the temple with them, walking and leaping and praising God. (Acts 3:2–8)

The church has a strong tradition, sometimes neglected in some churches, of anointing with oil or at least praying for those who are sick to be healed. From the *Book of Common Prayer*, we provide both the prayer over the oil and then the classic prayer for the sick:

> *O Lord, holy Father*, <u>giver of health and salvation</u>: **Send**
> **your Holy Spirit to sanctify this oil**; *that, as your holy*
> *apostles anointed many that were sick and healed them,*
> *so may those who in faith and repentance receive this holy*
> *unction be made whole*; through Jesus Christ our Lord, who
> lives and reigns with you and the Holy Spirit, one God, for
> ever and ever. *Amen.*

Some are not accustomed to the use of oil, but oil and healing prayer are a common occurrence in the Bible (Mark 6:13; Luke 10:34; James 5:14). Now the prayer for the sick:

> *Heavenly Father*, <u>giver of life and health</u>: **Comfort and**
> **relieve your sick servants, and give your power of**
> **healing to those who minister to their needs**, *that those*
> *[provide name] for whom our prayers are offered may be*
> *strengthened in their weakness and have confidence in*
> *your loving care*; through Jesus Christ our Lord, who lives
> and reigns with you and the Holy Spirit, one God, now and
> for ever. *Amen.*

These prayers are direct, they are clear, and they are fearless. Why? Because healing is what is wanted. Ask God for what you want.

Ask God for Faithfulness

The word "faith" translates the Greek term *pistis*, which as a verb is *pisteuo*, and that word is translated "believe." Faith has three senses in the New Testament: trust (as in trusting Christ for redemption, for healing), faithfulness (in the sense of allegiance to Christ over the time of our life), and faith (as the content of what we believe).[39] All of this and more appear in the church's prayer traditions, and they include petitions about doing what is right and following Christ and obedience and waiting or endurance.

Do you remember what Jesus prayed for Peter when both of them were looking into the furnace of death? Luke tells us: "Simon, Simon, listen! Satan has demanded to sift all of you like wheat, but I have prayed for you *that your own faith may not fail*; and you, when once you have turned back, strengthen your brothers" (Luke 22:31–32). The apostle Paul prayed for nothing less than robust faithfulness in a rich variety of expressions for the Colossians:

> For this reason, since the day we heard it, we have not ceased praying for you and asking **that you may be filled with the knowledge of God's will in all spiritual wisdom and understanding, so that you may lead lives worthy of the Lord, fully pleasing to him, as you bear fruit in every good work and as you grow in the knowledge of God. May you be made strong with all the strength that comes from his glorious power, and may you be prepared to endure everything with patience, while joyfully giving thanks to the Father**, who has enabled you to share in the inheritance of the saints in the light. He has rescued us from the power of darkness and transferred us into the kingdom of his beloved Son, in whom we have redemption, the forgiveness of sins. (Colossians 1:9–14)

On one of the Sundays after Pentecost we pray this fourfold form of faithfulness (Proper 17, reformatted):[40]

> *Lord of all power and might*, the author and giver of all good things:

Graft in our hearts the love of your Name;
increase in us true religion;
nourish us with all goodness;
and bring forth in us the fruit of good works;

through Jesus Christ our Lord, who lives and reigns with
you and the Holy Spirit, one God, for ever and ever. *Amen*

Ask God for Reverence and Holiness

The term *holiness* is not much in favor today, in part because of
the baggage that seems to accompany it. For many holiness is entirely
negative, if not little more than being picky about items like drinking or
daily devotions or rigorous disciplines, yet the term is entirely positive
in the Bible.[41] To begin with, God is holy, and God's holiness is one of
a kind. Wherever God is, that is where God is present, is holy. Holiness
then is about God's presence, and the Old Testament launches this theme
of God's presence in the tabernacle and in the temple. In addition to
holiness being about God's presence, the people of God are called to
holiness. Unfortunately, many think this term means "separateness,"
and that's true, but it's a half-truth, and half-truths distort. Holiness
for humans means, before separation, to be devoted to the one and only
holy God and God's presence. Thus, holiness means devotion to God,
and being devoted to God and to God's presence means separating from
worldliness and sinfulness. To be devoted to God is to be undevoted to
what is common and ordinary.

As Israelites became hesitant to pronounce the sacred name of God,
called the Tetragrammaton (the four-letter name of God), YHWH, and
wrote "Adonai" (Lord) instead of YHWH, so Jesus taught his followers in
his distinctive prayer to hallow or sanctify or reverence the Name of God
(Matthew 6:9). Jesus prayed that his disciples would be "sanctified," or
made holy (John 17:17). Paul's prayer for the Ephesians and Colossians,
both cited above, are all about this understanding of holiness. On Good
Friday many in the liturgical traditions devote themselves to holiness
in these words: "Give us grace so to put away the leaven of malice and

wickedness, that we may always serve you in pureness of living and truth" (*Book of Common Prayer*, Friday in Easter Week).

The proper posture for humans before the All-Holy God is reverence, humility, and bowing or kneeling. In our time on the island of Naxos, Greece, it was not uncommon to spot someone making the sign of the cross. I noticed, too, that it was because they themselves had observed either a church or a small shrine with a cross in it. In my reading of books about the church's prayers I found Frank Colquhoun's *Parish Prayers* filled with such petitions, like this one:

> *Almighty and eternal God,*
> **So draw our hearts to thee, so guide our minds, so fill our imaginations, so control our wills,**
> > *That we may be wholly thine, utterly dedicated unto thee;*
> > *And then use us, we pray thee, as thou wilt,*
> > *But always to thy glory and the welfare of thy people*;
> Through our Lord and Saviour Jesus Christ.[42]

Ask God for Love

Love is not as natural as we might think, especially love for God and love for our enemies. God is love, and our Trinitarian faith of Father, Son, and Spirit is a faith in a God who is a communion of love. This God of love loves us, and from God's love we learn to love others. Love is a rugged, affective commitment to another person to be with them, to be for them, and to grow with them into Christoformity.[43] Love then is both love for God and love for others in the sense of a rugged, affective commitment of presence, advocacy, and direction toward Christlikeness.

Jesus' high priestly prayer in John 17 finishes with his prayer that his followers may dwell in the love of the Father and Son: "I made your name known to them, and I will make it known, so that the love with which you have loved me may be in them, and I in them" (17:26). Paul, too, prayed that those in Thessalonica would learn to walk in love:

Now may our *God and Father himself and our Lord
Jesus* **direct our way to you. And may the** *Lord* **make
you increase and abound in love for one another and
for all, just as we abound in love for you. And may he
so strengthen your hearts in holiness that you may be
blameless before our God and Father at the coming of our
Lord Jesus with all his saints.** (1 Thessalonians 3:11–13)

The church has learned to pray the same: "Plant in every heart, we
pray, the love of him who is the Savior of the world, our Lord Jesus
Christ" (Holy Name Sunday, 1 January, *Book of Common Prayer*). Love
of God prompts love of others. A prayer that communicates love for
others, in this context for family members leaving the home for the day
or a season, is a Celtic blessing I have said many times:

> May the peace of the Lord Christ go with you,
> Wherever He may send you.
> May He guide you through the wilderness,
> Protect you through the storm.
> May He bring you home rejoicing
> At the wonders He has shown you.
> May He bring you home rejoicing
> Once again into our doors.[44]

Love is the fruit of the Spirit, so Spirit comes into a Collect on the
Seventh Sunday of the Epiphany: "O Lord . . . Send your Holy Spirit and
pour into our hearts your greatest gift, which is love, the true bond of
peace and of all virtue, without which whoever lives is accounted dead
before you."

What we Ask God could go on and on, but I will give one more, the
seventh item.

Ask God for the Holy Spirit

Starting with Jesus in John 20 when Jesus "breathed on" the disciples and said, "Receive the Holy Spirit" to the great day of Pentecost when the Spirit came down like fire (Acts 2) to Peter and John laying hands on those in Samaria to receive the Spirit (Acts 8:14–17) to Paul praying for Apollos to receive the Spirit (Acts 19:1–7), the church learned the practice, sometimes accompanied again with anointing with oil, of praying for the Spirit to come on themselves and others.

On the Seventh Sunday after the Epiphany those using the *Book of Common Prayer* ask the Lord to "Send your Holy Spirit and pour into our hearts your greatest gift, which is love, the true bond of peace and of all virtue, without which whoever lives is accounted dead before you." We ask this because we are incapable of living this kind of love apart from God's gracious gift of the Spirit.

On the Seventh Sunday of Easter, which is the Sunday after the Ascension, at which time Christ was taken from his followers, we recall their sorrow as a starting point for reunion with him: "O God, the King of glory, you have exalted your only Son Jesus Christ with great triumph to your kingdom in heaven: Do not leave us comfortless, but send us your Holy Spirit to strengthen us, and exalt us to that place where our Savior Christ has gone before."

During the Season after Pentecost we pray for God to "Grant us the grace of your Holy Spirit, that we may be devoted to you with our whole heart, and united to one another with pure affection" (Proper 9). God's power brings unity by the Spirit: "Grant, O merciful God, that your Church, being gathered together in unity by your Holy Spirit, may show forth your power among all peoples, to the glory of your Name" (Proper 16).

7

REMIND GOD

I f the first question in composing a biblically patterned petition is "What do I/we want?," the second question is, "What about God makes what I/we want something God would want to answer?" This question leads us into the deep theological roots of prayer: What about God makes God want to answer this prayer request? Put differently, in the Remind God element we anchor our requests in truths about God in such a way that it is consistent with God to answer the prayer request.

Reminding God emerges in some of the earliest prayers of the Bible. This long prayer by David in 2 Samuel 7:18–29 is as theologically profound as it is a template for how the pattern of petition took shape in the Bible and then was developed in the church. I will mark this prayer as I have marked others:

> Then King David went in and sat before the LORD, and said, "Who am I, *O Lord GOD*, and what is my house, that you have brought me thus far? And yet this was a small thing in your eyes, *O Lord GOD*; you have spoken also of your servant's house for a great while to come. **May this be instruction for the people,** *O Lord GOD*! And what more can David say to you? For you know your servant, *O Lord GOD*!
>
> Because of your promise, and according to your own heart, you have wrought all this greatness, so that your servant may know it. Therefore you are great, *O LORD God*; for there is no one like you, and there is no God besides you, according to all that we have heard with our ears. Who is

like your people, like Israel? Is there another nation on earth whose God went to redeem it as a people, and to make a name for himself, doing great and awesome things for them, by driving out before his people nations and their gods? And you established your people Israel for yourself to be your people forever; and you, O Lᴏʀᴅ, became their God.

And now, *O Lᴏʀᴅ God*, **as for the word that you have spoken concerning your servant and concerning his house, confirm it forever; do as you have promised**.

Thus your name will be magnified forever in the saying, 'The Lᴏʀᴅ of hosts is God over Israel'; and the house of your servant David will be established before you. For you, O Lᴏʀᴅ of hosts, the God of Israel, have made this revelation to your servant, saying, 'I will build you a house'; therefore your servant has found courage to pray this prayer to you.

And now, *O Lord Gᴏᴅ*, you are God, and your words are true, and you have promised this good thing to your servant; **now therefore may it please you to bless the house of your servant, so that it may continue forever before you**; for you, *O Lord Gᴏᴅ*, have spoken, and with your blessing shall the house of your servant be blessed forever."

God, he is saying, should answer his petitions because God is faithful and God desires to be glorified in his world. As Abraham and Jacob and Moses and Solomon reminded God of who God has been, who God is, and what God has done, so David does too. He Asks God for relatively little here compared with the theological portrait he paints of God: "confirm it [the Expectations] forever; do as you have promised" with "bless the house of your servant." This, along with Solomon's lengthy Remind God section, becomes in Judaism, in Jesus ("who are in heaven," etc.), in the apostles, and then in the Collect tradition of the church a powerful pattern to anchor one's requests in the very nature and actions of God.

I add to this biblical example three quick examples in *The Book of Common Prayer* that illustrate the Remind God element of the pattern of petitions:

> O God, the strength of all who put their trust in you (Sixth Sunday after Epiphany);

> Almighty Father, whose dear Son, on the night before he suffered, instituted the Sacrament of his Body and Blood (Maundy Thursday);

> Almighty God, the foundation of all wisdom, you know our necessities before we ask and our ignorance in asking (Season after Pentecost, Proper 11).

Pausing Long Enough to Remind God

We need to learn to do this and here's why: our prayers tend to Address God and then immediately launch without pause into the Ask God element. We have grown neglectful of the Remind God element that is so clear in both the Bible and in the church's Collect tradition. Janet Morley, a well-known writer of prayers, wrote a prayer for the Third Sunday after Pentecost that illustrates the more biblical pattern:[45]

> Christ *our teacher*,
> *you urge us beyond all reason*
> *to love our enemies,*
> *and pray for our oppressors.*
> May we embrace such folly
> not through subservience, but strength;
> that unmeasured generosity
> may be poured into our lap,
> through Jesus Christ. **Amen.**

The Remind God element in the pattern of petitions shapes us in our praying into well-rounded theology. It is the case that most of the time we don't pause to acknowledge the greatness or goodness or graciousness of God when we pray. We say "Father," and we immediately get down to the business of our petition. Yes, at times that is appropriate, but not always. We might learn a more appropriate way to pray by giving more attention to truths about God when we pray. We might, then, learn to ponder God directly when we address God. In fact, prayers in the Bible and church tradition have a habit of reminding God of who God is and what God has done. As Samuel Wells and Abigail Kocher put it in their wonderful book *Shaping the Prayers of the People*, these truths about God are "an appeal to God to keep to a track record and act in character."[46] Yes, "track record." That's what the Remind God element does.

Anglicans join others who pray the Collects, but there is an emphasis in the Anglican way that needs to mentioned. It is often stated in the Latin line *lex orandi, lex credendi*, which roughly translates, "the law of prayer is the law of faith."[47] Put less woodenly, we learn our theology in praying, and our praying expresses our theology. Our worship is our theology, and our theology is our worship.[48] No one said this more memorably than Evagrius of Pontus, a famous (Eastern) Orthodox monk: "If you are a theologian, you will pray truly. And if you pray truly, you are a theologian."[49] Evagrius here does not have in mind the modern professor theologian but the ancient monastic theologian who spent his or her time in disciplined prayer and spiritual practices. True theology is not the academic life of theoretical puzzles but a life of worship. I am at times asked, "What do Anglicans believe?" and I respond with "Join us for worship for a few months and that will answer your question." Aidan Kavanagh points us in the right direction when he observes that "The worship and belief of Christians converge, meet, entwine, and meld in their liturgical act."[50] Charles Hefling, an expert on all things Anglican, sums it up this way:

> Other churches may be anchored in confessional documents,
> or doctrinal formularies, or a systematically articulated

theology, or the pronouncements of magisterial authorities. Anglicans—so they are wont to say—are different. The Anglican anchor is worship.[51]

Theologians know these Collects are a gold mine of Christian theology, and the Remind God element is at the heart of that theology. But this must be said again lest we lose our way into some clique: the Collects were not invented by Anglicans. They are the deposit of the Bible's and the church's tradition of learning how to petition God.

Four Themes to Remind God

At this point one could pause to read and summarize a fat book about God in order to grasp the fullness of what can be said as we Remind God. What follows is based on the Bible and the Collects during the season after Pentecost (Ordinary Time) as well as some prayers by others closer to our time. These will bring to the surface central themes about God that we can use to anchor our Ask God petitions in a Remind God set of lines. In the Collects during the weeks after Pentecost, which are some of the most well-known and memorized, we remind God about God's works. The season begins on Trinity Sunday and finishes on Christ the King Sunday. We remind God over and over that

> God is a God of grace,
> God is good,
> God redeems us in Christ, and
> our Lord Jesus is on the throne.

We Remind God of these themes during this season, and these themes anchor our petitions and determine, as we will see in the next chapter, which Address for God we will use.

Remind God that God is Gracious

Sometimes we Ask God for something that leads in our musings to
the realization that *if* God gives us what we want, it will be because of
God's grace. Grace, commonly understood as God's goodness toward
undeserving sinners, is the major theme of the weeks after Pentecost's
Collects. A recent study by John Barclay puts grace on a new level of
understanding, and it provides a deeper sense of our petitions. Barclay
begins his study with how "gift" is understood among anthropologists,
and he shows that *a gift always connects the giver and the gift into a
special relationship of mutual obligation.* The implication is obvious:
God's gift to us in Christ forges a relational bond between us and so
obligates us to thanksgiving and faithfulness. Barclay then examines
gift and grace in the ancient texts—Greek, Roman, and Jewish—and
in the history of the church. He concludes this must-read, magisterial
study with six themes of grace, or gift, with respect to the giver and the
recipient. Here are his clipped summaries for each theme:[52]

(1) **superabundance**: the supreme scale, lavishness, or
permanence of the gift;
(2) **singularity**: the attitude of the giver as marked solely
and purely by benevolence;
(3) **priority**: the timing of the gift before the recipient's
initiative;
(4) **incongruity**: the distribution of the gift without regard to
the worth of the recipient;
(5) **efficacy**: the impact of the gift on the nature or agency of
the recipient;
(6) **non-circularity**: the escape of the gift from an ongoing
cycle of reciprocity.

Barclay's study has many implications, but perhaps the first is that
grace/gift has more than one simple theme such as "God's gift at Christ's
expense." Or as "it's all free." Grace might emphasize the magnificence

of the gift, or that God alone is always gracious, or that God acts first, or that God's gift to us and our worthiness are not at all congruent, or that God's grace is a power that transforms, or that grace means we accept and that's it (pure gift). It is important, even in studying the so-called apostle of grace, Paul, that one or more of these themes can be present without all of them being present. Barclay contends that it is rare that all six are present in any given author. Grace, then, is a term with many possible evocations, and it does not then always reduce itself to "pure" gift (#6 above). Grace is a theme we need to use to anchor our Ask God petitions.

Grace is all about God the giver of all good things; this prayer by Walter Brueggemann highlights our giving God:[53]

You God of command who issues demands upon us;
You God of Expectations who compels us to hope;
You God of deliverance endlessly up-ending our systems of abuse;
In all your commanding, your promising, your delivering,
   We notice your *giving*.
   Indeed your giving is what we notice first, best, and most,
     about your own life . . .
     giving without reserve or limitation.
You give us worlds of beauty and abundance,
     blessed and fruitful,
You give us sustenance for the day,
     so that we are not smitten by the sun by day
       or the moon by night.
You give us – in the center of all your giving –
   your only, well-beloved Son.
You give us your spirit of power, energy, and wisdom.
     Gifts all without grudging!
And we receive, because we have no alternative,
     because we cannot live without your gifts,
       because we have nothing but what you have given us.

We receive, carefully and anxiously,
    worried that there is not enough,
        of security and safety,
        of grades or grants or dollars or friends,
            of sex or beer or SUVs,
                or students and endowments,
            of futures, and so we crave and store up for rainy futures.
We receive occasionally when you stagger us
  and we break beyond anxiety,
    in gratitude,
        recognizing that you in your generosity give us
           more than enough,
  and in grateful giving we become our true selves,
    breathed in the image of your Son.
So we ponder your generosity and we are dazzled.
We measure our gratitude and our capacity to be generous.
  We pray your haunting us beyond ourselves,
    in wonder at your way,
    in love for the world you love,
    in praise that transforms our fear,
    in wonder, love, and praise,
        our lives beyond ourselves,
        toward you,
        a blessing in the world.
Hear us we pray in the name of the emptied, exalted One. Amen.

A chapel prayer / September 20, 2001

Grace, then, is about God's giving—abundantly, generously, diversely, receptively—and Brueggemann's prayer shows that we "cannot live" apart from God's own gifts to us and that without those gifts we have nothing.

The Collect tradition of the church's petitions about God's grace emphasizes our undeserved gifts, or what Barclay calls "incongruity." God gives us both what we don't deserve and more than what we deserve.

The centurion who wanted his servant healed knew if it happened it would be out of the powerful grace of Jesus's God:

> The centurion answered, "Lord, I am not worthy to have
> you come under my roof; but only speak the word, and my
> servant will be healed." (Matthew 8:8)

What he got he knew was from God's grace, not from his own deserving.

So, in Proper 1 we ask God to "Remember, O Lord, what you have wrought in us and not what we deserve." Proper 14 expresses conviction that grace determines our existence and our obedience when it says, "Grant to us, Lord, we pray, the spirit to think and do always those things that are right, that we, who cannot exist without you, may by you be enabled to live according to your will." Proper 19 is not far from this when it begins, "O God, because without you we are not able to please you." This theme of God's grace behind all we do that pleases God, which can be found in Paul's letters in passages such as Ephesians 2:8–9, comes to expression yet again in these words: "Almighty and merciful God, it is only by your gift that your faithful people offer you true and laudable service" (Proper 26). God's grace is a feature in the Remind God element in a biblically cased petition. We remind God about God's own unmeasurable grace, and we remind God that we don't deserve it.

Remind God that God is Good

Another theme in which to anchor our Ask God petitions is God's utter goodness.

God's superabundant grace is manifested in God's sheer goodness. God, we muse as we ponder our petitions, should answer our petitions because God is altogether Good. Goodness or good translate the Hebrew word *tov*. The psalmist declares it: "You are *tov* and do *tov*" (Psalm 119:68). When God chose to reveal his glory to Moses, he hid Moses in a crag and said, "I will make all my *tov* pass before you, and will proclaim before you the name, 'The LORD'; and I will be gracious to whom I will be gracious, and will show mercy on whom I will show mercy" (Exodus 33:19). God's *tov* passes by Moses, with God's palm protecting Moses, and when God's *tov* passes by God announces his name, YHWH. God's name and God's *tov* are virtual synonyms.

There's more to consider here: God **is** *tov* but God also **does** *tov.* We observe how often goodness is present in the prayers of the Book of Psalms. "Yes, *tov* and faithful love will pursue me all the days of my life" (Psalm 23:6, CEB). Don't miss this: God relentlessly and tenaciously chases us with *tov.* So the psalmist says aloud to all who will listen what our Relentless-*Tov*-God does in us when God captures us: "O taste and see that the LORD is *tov*" (34:8). Those who tasted this *tov* can also say "But for me it is *tov* to be near God" (73:28). One more: "For you, O Lord, are good [*tov*] and forgiving, abounding in steadfast love to all who call on you" (86:5).

A third theme about God's goodness will further support anchoring our Ask God petitions. *Tov* is God's design for all creation. We can Ask God for something good to happen because God created all things good. Everything is shaped by God for goodness. God's turning the "formless and empty" into created order gave everything created a design, a purpose, a function. God looks at his own creation and shouts with echoes into the deeps of the universe with *Tov*! *Tov* is about beauty, about what satisfies both what we see and what we hear.

Singer, songwriter, and speaker Rachel Barrentine has composed a beautiful prayer that affirms over and over that God is *tov.*[54]

> Dear Lord,
> Though circumstances look dreary,
> Though storms are raging,
> **You are still good.**
>
> Though wars are waging,
> Though darkness is encroaching,
> **You are still good.**

Though my hope is weary,
Though my heart is exhausted,
You are still good.

In every difficulty,
In every question mark,
You are still good.

I declare Your goodness on the peaks.
I declare Your goodness in the pit.
You are still good.

Now Lord, be my Remembrance.
In the moments of heartache,
In the miles of wilderness,
In the marrow of the unknown,
You are still good.

In Jesus' name, identity, and character I pray,
Amen.

Three Collects in the season after Pentecost speak of the goodness of God in a way that anchors our petitions. In Proper 5, we pray, "O God, from whom all good proceeds," while in Proper 17 we acknowledge the "Lord of all power and might" who is "the author and giver of all good things." My favorite goodness Collect appears in the *Book of Common Prayer* in Proper 22: "Almighty and everlasting God, you are always more ready to hear than we to pray, and to give more than we either desire or deserve." That is sheer goodness: God is ready to hear from us and God will give more than we even desire (or deserve).

In our petitions it is good to Remind God that God is good. In praying in this pattern, we are formed into people who know God as good, who learn the goodness of God, and who have learned to expect God to be good. So, we have courage to Ask God because we have learned that God is good.

Remind God that God Redeems Us in Christ

The essential act of God's grace, the essential gift, is Christ, who was sent for our redemption. This too is an anchor for our petitions. The church's many prayers during the season after Pentecost remind God that God redeems in Christ. We begin with the opening lines of Moses' famous song in Exodus 15:

> Then Moses and the Israelites sang this song to the Lord:
>
> "I will sing to the Lord, for he has triumphed gloriously;
>> horse and rider he has thrown into the sea.
> The Lord is my strength and my might,
>> and he has become my salvation;
> this is my God, and I will praise him,
>> my father's God, and I will exalt him.
> The Lord is a warrior;
>> the Lord is his name. (15:1–3)

At the other end of the Bible we find another song, the song of the four living beasts and twenty-four elders in Revelation 5, who like Moses sing of God's redemption:

> They took up a new song, saying,
>
> "You are worthy to take the scroll and open its seals,
>> because you were slain,
>> and by your blood you purchased for God
>>> persons from every tribe, language, people, and nation.
> You made them a kingdom and priests to our God,
>> and they will rule on earth." (5:9–10, CEB)

When it comes to the element of Reminding God about redemption, the church's Collects stand out. In the middle of the season after Pentecost, somewhere in the middle of August, we acknowledge God's redemption in God's Son by affirming aloud with one another for all to hear, "you have given your only Son to be for us a sacrifice for sin," and, because in this season of the calendar Christ as an example is emphasized, we also say the Son is "an example of godly life" (Proper 15).

Christ as example, sometimes called *imitatio Christi* (imitation of Christ), is grounded not only in Jesus' call to follow him (Luke 9:23) but also in the apostle Paul's own words when he taught his churches this: "Follow my example, as I follow the example of Christ" (1 Corinthians 11:1, NIV). Recent studies by Michael Gorman have centered the vision of discipleship in the term "cruciformity," or being conformed to the cross of Christ (as Jesus himself taught).[55] He's right, and I have myself proposed that we could label this just as well "Christoformity,"[56] because redemption in Christ is God's act for us and in us so we might be conformed to the image of the Son (Romans 8:29). Christoformity is not, however, a pulling tight the belt buckle and giving an extra shove but instead something that flows from redemptive grace. As Barbee and Zahl put it, this prayer (Proper 15 again) "invokes the Atonement as the foundation of our living out concretely a Christ-like life."[57]

Near the end of the season after Pentecost, we acknowledge again the truth about God's redemption in Christ: "whose blessed Son came into the world that he might destroy the works of the devil and make us children of God and heirs of eternal life" (Proper 27). Notice that once again redemption is fashioned as the gracious, prior, and efficacious act of God to destroy evil at the cross and through that act to place us in God's family and to provide for us life beyond that now-defeated death.

If the Collects acknowledge God as the one who sent the Son for our redemption, we also are taught to Remind God another truth about God: God's providence or divine plan. We say God orders all of creation: "O God, your never-failing providence sets in order all things both in heaven and earth" (Proper 4). During the season after Pentecost we publicly and verbally participate in the truth that our God is a God who redeems, who has made redemption for all, and who calls us to conformity to the Christ of this redemption. Through God's grace and the gift of the Spirit, as we continue to Remind God about God, we are conformed into a people redeemed who are on mission to offer this redemption to all.

Remind God that Christ is Lord

The church's calendar closes the season after Pentecost on Christ the King Sunday, a fitting finale to a season that began with Trinity Sunday. The One-in-Three God is supremely revealed in the Son, and this Son is nothing less the world's true ruler, so we address God as "Almighty and everlasting God" and we acknowledge this truth about God: "whose will it is to restore all things in your well-beloved Son, the King of kings and Lord of lords" (Proper 29). The deeper this Collect penetrates our hearts the more we will be formed into people whose ruler is not the president of the United States but the one who died, who has defeated evil, who was raised, who rules from the throne of God, and who will come again, which is what Advent is all about.

And, yet . . . I never pray this Collect at the end of the church calendar without wondering When and Why and Why not now? When will the Lord who reigns end injustice? Why does our Ruler not rule more in line with what we know to be God's will? And, why not do this now? The following prayer from Walter Brueggemann takes us there on Christ the King Sunday; this prayer flows so forcefully from the Psalms and also focuses both on the name of the Address and the Truths about God that God will be reminded of:

> Blessed are [sic] thou, king of the universe!
> We name you king, lord, master, governor
> and by such naming we relieve our deep anxieties
> in confidence at your rule.
> And yet ... we notice your stunning irrelevance
> to the issues of the day
> that require hands-on attention.
> We name you king and pray daily for your coming kingdom,
> And yet ... we also notice you creep over
> into violence and oppressive demand.
> We name you king and loudly proclaim that your messiah
> will come again, come soon, in glory and power.

And yet ... all the while, we grow weary
with the brutal powers of the day.
We name you king and wait for your show of
vulnerability and mercy and compassion
that will "new" the world and heal our common life.
We name you, and we wait ... but not patiently.
Blessed art thou, king of the universe! Amen.[58]

On reading 1 Samuel 8 / March 4, 1999

The church's prayer tradition begins in the Bible and flows into every church stream to become the way the church prays. One of the most consistent elements of the pattern of petitionary prayer is to Remind God of truths about God in order to ground our petitions in God's ways and God's very nature. Our focus so far has been on the core elements (Ask God, Remind God), so we turn to the third element of the pattern (Expect God).

8

EXPECT GOD

There are five elements in the church's development of the Bible's pattern of petitionary prayer. As a template for our own requests they offer to us the Bible's and the church's wisdom on learning to ask God for something. The questions we ask are these: What do we want? What about God makes answering this prayer God-like? And now we turn to What do we expect to occur if God answers our request? What we expect varies from petition to petition. It can be a hope, a promise, or a transformation of us, but the word *Expect* attempts to put all these (and more) into a tight bundle. The classic term in prayer books is "Aspiration."

Now an oddity: most written prayers and very few verbal prayers in my hearing have learned to use the Expect God element of Bible-based and church tradition prayers. So our fund of instruction in this chapter will be the Collects. But notice this from Jesus:

> So they took away the stone. And Jesus looked upward and said, "*Father*, I thank you for having heard me. I knew that you always hear me, but I have said this for the sake of the crowd standing here, *so that they may believe that you sent me.*" (John 11:41–42)

In their book on helping us to learn to pray, Wells and Kocher clarify the Expect God element in this way. The various expectations "proceed to describe the outcome the speaker imagines, often in terms of the change to the speaker him- or herself and to the community."[59] Our Expect God is their "outcome." These expectations or outcomes, they observe, need to be specific, they need space for celebrating the answers, and they at times can be almost too good—so they point to three provisos in framing the goal of our petitions:

> A personal and pious climax to a petition is often moving, lyrical, and empowering and has many advantages, so long as three provisos are borne in mind. First, that this is not the invariable climax to the prayer — but instead is one of a variety of ways of concluding. Second, that this section is brief and does not take too much attention away from the primary focus, which should be the persons and places mentioned in the primary petition and the imperative verbs throughout. Third, that its attention is directed towards making the church a community of character and witness rather than making the individual fit for heaven.[60]

As we learn to ask God for what we really want we can strengthen the Ask God and the Expect God elements by thinking about *Why* we want what we are asking. This takes our petition from *just wanting* to *wanting for a purpose consistent with divine purposes*.

We turn now to five themes in the Expect God to answer element. These five themes can become considerations us for in two ways: first, we can probe introspectively into *Why* we want something from God and, second, we can learn to baptize our goals into the church's wisdom as it has formed the Expect God (or Aspiration) of our petitions. The church tradition—from the earliest centuries on—has been Eucharistic in emphasizing the Lord's Supper as the high point of the assembled people of God, so it is not surprising that a primary theme of the goal is forgiveness of sin.

Forgiveness

If you have sinned as you approach God or the Eucharist table— and it would be more accurate to say, "Since you have sinned"—then approaching God in confession and petition for forgiveness is a common experience. I remember as a teenager asking a friend if he had ever asked God to forgive him. His answer was one I was not prepared to respond to. He said, "I do that every Sunday." I was a saved Baptist, so I had done the forgiveness part once-for-all, and the idea of getting forgiveness each week jarred my thinking. Only later was I able to connect the need for regular forgiveness—in the style of 1 John 1:9—with the Eucharist focus of many churches, and only then was I also able to see that learning to live in a way that is consistent with God's gracious forgiveness is remembering and reliving the redemption in Christ.

On Ash Wednesday we address God as "Almighty and everlasting God," and we remind God of this: "you hate nothing you have made and forgive the sins of all who are penitent." This leads to the simple petition for God to "Create and make in us new and contrite hearts." All this leads to the Expect God element: "**that** we, worthily lamenting our sins and acknowledging our wretchedness, **may obtain of you,** the God of all mercy, **perfect remission and forgiveness**." Again, it is not that we don't believe we have been forgiven or that God is holding over us some threat of taking forgiveness away. Rather, we re-participate and embody in memory this great benefit of our gospel that we have already received and that we re-member as we participate in Eucharist.

This theme of finding forgiveness is perhaps the most prominent theme in the widest circles of the church's prayer tradition, and I hasten to add that this is especially emphatic in the Eastern Orthodox prayer tradition. This theme can give our own prayers for forgiveness a clearer sight line.

Eternal Life

As one who grew up in the evangelical and fundamentalist register, I find the regular appearance of a petition leading toward eternal life comes as a surprise. "Isn't this already settled?" was the question I asked as I first encountered this hope for eternal life in the church's prayers. But eternal life in the Expect God element of petition is found often in all branches of the church prayer tradition as one of the expected results of our petitions. When one adds up the themes of the Expect God in the

Collects used for ordinary services[61] one might be surprised how often eternal life, or something like it, comes to expression. It is not that the people of God are unsure about the work of God. Rather, the Expect God element in petitions expresses our deepest and ultimate hope.

I begin on a Celtic note. The Celtic prayer tradition used many compline or nighttime prayers that were said as a person went to bed. Darkness was connected in those days with death and fear of death and evil spirits and temptations, so a rich bedtime prayer developed, including this compline prayer of Felgild of Farne (eighth century), throughout which this theme of eternal life is implied, though it is not once mentioned:

> I will lie down this night with God,
> and God will lie down with me;
> I will lie down this night with Christ,
> and Christ will lie down with me;
> I will lie down this night with the Spirit,
> and the Spirit will lie down with me;
> God and Christ and the Spirit, be lying down with me.[62]

This one is complemented by the compline prayer of Boisil, a seventh-century monk:

> I am placing my soul and my body
> in Thy safe keeping this night, O God,
> in Thy safe keeping, O Jesus Christ,
> in Thy safe keeping, O Spirit of perfect truth.
> The Three who would defend my cause
> be keeping me this night from harm.[63]

The Expect God element both in some biblical prayers as well as in the church Collect tradition begins almost always with the word "that." So, our template Collect for Purity instructs us again:

Almighty God,

to you all hearts are open,
all desires known,
and from you no secrets are hid:

Cleanse the thoughts of our hearts
by the inspiration of your Holy Spirit,

that we may perfectly love you,
and worthily magnify your holy Name;

through Christ our Lord.
Amen.

The church calendar opens Advent's First Sunday with the hope rooted in the grace of abandoning sins and affirming the "armor of light," and here is what is expected when God answers the prayer: "**that** in the last day, when he shall come again in his glorious majesty to judge both the living and the dead, we may rise to the life immortal." The one praying this Collect desires holiness because that kind of person will "rise to the life immortal." It is important to emphasize that ridding ourselves of sin is not the point, and neither is living a life of holiness, but the expectation is rather attaining to eternal life. In this way our discipline to become holy is not the goal but rather the way of life that prepares for something far greater: life immortal. A few more examples now.

On Easter the petition itself is for God's grace "to die daily to sin," and this too is extended to a more ultimate end: "**that** we may evermore live with him in the joy of his resurrection." There is no resurrection without death, but death is not an end but a means to new life.

The Sixth Sunday of Easter's Ask God element is "Pour into our hearts such love towards you" and the Expect God to answer that petition is "**that** we, loving you in all things and above all things, may obtain your promises, which exceed all that we can desire." This is language about heaven, while it is also language about what can be known now in part.

Ultimate acceptance with God comes out during the Season after Pentecost with this: "**that** we may be made a holy temple acceptable to you" (Proper 8). The final end of Christoformity, rooted as noted already in Romans 8:29, becomes the Expect God element in Proper 27: "**that**, when he comes again with power and great glory, we may be made like him in his eternal and glorious kingdom."

World Evangelism

The church's petitions often expect an answer that leads to world evangelism, and this is sometimes tied to the sacraments. If in the bread and wine we encounter God's gracious redemption, then those same tokens of grace may well prompt us to think of those in need of redemption. On the Second Week after the Epiphany the Ask God element is that we, "illumined by your Word and Sacraments, may shine with the radiance of Christ's glory" so (now the Expect God element) "**that** he may be known, worshiped, and obeyed to the ends of the earth." The Third Sunday says it again: "**that** we and the whole world may perceive the glory of his marvelous works." During the Season after Pentecost we hear something quite similar about evangelism: "**that** through your grace we may proclaim your truth with boldness, and minister your justice with compassion" (Proper 6). But it is at Pentecost that we hear this theme the clearest, so here is the entire Collect reformatted into its elements:

Almighty God,

on this day you opened the way of eternal life
to every race and nation
by the promised gift of your Holy Spirit:

**Shed abroad this gift throughout the world
by the preaching of the Gospel**,

that it may reach to the ends of the earth;

through Jesus Christ our Lord,
who lives and reigns with you,
in the unity of the Holy Spirit,
one God,
for ever and ever.
Amen.

The hope is that gospel preaching about Jesus as Lord and Savior will blanket the entire world.

A pastoral observation: the Expect God element in the pattern of petitionary prayer has the capacity to form us into those who desire for the gospel to spread into the whole world. Sad to say, some have little more than vaporous aspirations when they utter these words. Some think evangelism is colonialism, some think it is arrogance, and some think it is for someone else—perhaps those revivalist evangelicals. One must say this because it is true: those uttering these Collects are often not known for evangelism, and this can only mean their utterings of these are not letting them be formative. I am profoundly grateful for my Bishop, Todd Hunter, of C4SO's diocese,[64] for his commitment to and practice of evangelism, for his commitment to and nurturing of church planting, and thus for his embodiment of the Expect God element in the petitions.

Christoformity

The expectation of the petitions of parents, churches, and pastors is to nurture Christoformity in families, churches, and in the personal life. To delineate this a bit in more detail, to be Christoform is to be like Christ, and that means to live as Christ lived, to die with Christ, to be raised with Christ, and to rule with Christ. If those are elements in the life of Christ then those are elements in our life. Even more, it is to be so baptized into the life, death, and resurrection of Christ that we find our way into a life like that of Jesus. It is to participate in Christ through the indwelling Spirit shaping us into a life like Christ's.

We often pray this in connection to the Eucharist. On the Fourth Sunday in Lent our petition is "Evermore give us this bread" with this as the Expect God to answer it: "**that** he may live in us, and we in him." Ingesting that bread, then, is to join in communion with who Christ is and what Christ has done. We ask on Palm Sunday for God's grace "**that** we may walk in the way of his suffering, and also share in his resurrection," and on Tuesday of Holy Week "**that** we may gladly suffer shame and loss for the sake of your Son our Savior Jesus Christ." And on the Fifth Sunday of Easter our petition is that God may "Grant us so perfectly to know your Son Jesus Christ to be the way, the truth, and the life," thereby leading us to this hope: "**that** we may steadfastly follow his steps in the way that leads to eternal life."

Live Faithfully Now

The largest theme in the Expect God (to answer our prayers) pertains to living the Christian life faithfully, in the here and now, a theme in the history of the Christian tradition that often finds expression in pleasing God. So, on the Sixth Sunday after the Epiphany, the Goal is "**that** in keeping your commandments we may please you both in will and deed." Along this line we ask God to preserve us from fears and anxieties "**that** no clouds of this mortal life may hide from us the light of that love which is immortal, and which you have manifested to us in your Son Jesus Christ our Lord" (Eighth Week after the Epiphany). A goal of a petition worthy of memorizing goes like this: "**that**, among the swift and varied changes of the world, our hearts may surely there be fixed where true joys are to be found" (Fifth Sunday of Lent).

"Grant us the grace of your Holy Spirit," the church prayer tradition teaches us to pray during the season after Pentecost, and that is followed by this goal: "**that** we may be devoted to you with our whole heart, and united to one another with pure affection" (Proper 9). Some weeks later the goal strengthens the previous one: "**that** your grace may always precede and follow us, that we may continually be given to good works" (Proper 23). Again, this is not just for us as individuals but for us as the Body of Christ, and we remind ourselves in Proper 24 "**that** your Church throughout the world may persevere with steadfast faith in the confession of your Name."

Finale

I'm a professor who teaches the Bible, and at the end of the Season after Pentecost we pray one of my favorite Collects:

Blessed Lord, <u>who caused all holy Scriptures to be written for our learning</u>: **Grant us so to hear them, read, mark, learn, and inwardly digest them,** *that we may embrace and ever hold fast the blessed hope of everlasting life, which you have given us in our Savior Jesus Christ*; who lives and reigns with you and the Holy Spirit, one God, for ever and ever. *Amen.* (Proper 28)

Scripture reading and teaching have an end beyond the knowing and growing and learning and teaching. It is "that we may embrace and ever hold fast the blessed hope of everlasting life, which you have given us in our Savior Jesus Christ."

The core of the Bible-shaped and church-based pattern for petitionary prayer has now been explained: Ask God, Remind God, and Expect God (to answer the petition). We need now to turn to the Address God element, and then we'll study the Access God.

9

ADDRESS GOD

The Addresses we use for God are shaped by the Bible. The Old Testament prayers, as seen in chapter one, are basically God, Lord, Lord God, LORD (=Yahweh, YHWH), and LORD God. As we noted in chapter two, these shift with Jesus into the church to "Father" and "Our Father" and "Our heavenly Father," but Father is the Address Jesus gave to his followers, and it has been the Address ever since. Some with a more theological twist to their prayers will begin their prayers today with "Father, Son, and Holy Spirit," but that too is a clear Christian rendering of the New Testament's theology.

One of the America's most influential Old Testament scholars is Walter Brueggemann, and his prayers before class were so valued that his students began to record them; some of them were eventually published in a book called *Awed to Heaven, Rooted in Earth*. Nothing in his prayers is more distinctive than the Remind God element that he brings to the surface as he opens his prayer and petitions. I record but one here, and you can see his emphasis on reminding God of both who God is and what God has done in the past:[65]

> You are the One who has brought our Lord Jesus Christ
> again to life from the dead;
> You are the One who by your summoning imperative
> has caused the worlds to be;
> You are the One who by your faithfulness
> has given a son to our vexed mother Hannah;
> You are the One who has the will and power to begin again,
> to start anew.

You are the only self-starter whose name we know.

And so we bid you, start again,

start here, start now,

start with us and with our school,

start with your mercy,

and with your justice,

and with your compassion,

and with your peace.

Make the world new again, and young again, and innocent again...

Start... before it is too late. Amen.

On reading 1 Samuel 1 / February 4, 1999

Prayer requires a "theo-logy," and it would be wise for us to ponder Who God is and What God has done before we pray, not least when we are composing our own Collects. This Remind God element, I am pressing us to see, determines which title we give God in the Address God element of the petition.

One of my teachers in seminary was Murray Harris, a brilliant New Testament scholar with a deep personal piety. His New Zealand accent was no doubt an attraction, but that accent was transcended by his devotion when he prayed to open class. Murray was not an Anglican, but he learned to pray with near perfection when compared to the biblical and church tradition of petitions. He always began the prayer with enough silence to quiet us all and to usher in reverence before our God. He would then address God with terms like "Father" or "Our Father," and then he opened up the address with "you" or "who" or "in whom" or "in whose" in such a way that the God addressed was spelled out, defined, and articulated in such a manner as to lead to the petition he was about to make for God to guide, nourish, strengthen, and illumine our minds as we studied God's Word. Sometimes the petition was more than one, and he finished with some kind of word about our sole access through Christ in the Spirit, like "Through Christ our Lord, Amen." One doesn't have to be Anglican or steeped in the prayer books to see the biblical wisdom of this pattern of prayer.

The second, third, and fourth elements of the pattern (Remind God, Ask God, Expect God to answer) give rise to the Address we use for God. When you pray what do you call God? To name God is to describe both who God is and to clarify our relationship to God. We need to take (more) seriously what terms we use for God when we pray. One might say the Address we use brings to expression the whole prayer. Or, to put that idea into a twist, "So, to paraphrase, the way in which God is addressed in worship is what settles the convictions that worshippers adopt and hold about the God they address."[66] In composing our own Collects or in learning to pray, if we begin (as I suggested in the previous chapter) with Ask God and then Remind God with an eye toward Expect God . . . if we are working backwards, the name we use to address God fits the whole prayer.

Yes, of course, our prayers are at times musings. We may open with "Father" and then think about God and then ask God and then think about God some more, and then address God again, and then ask God . . . you get the picture. Yes, this is not uncommon to our own prayers. But earlier in this book we focused on the essentials of the pattern of petition in the Bible and the church tradition's Collect, and we turn then to the Address in that tradition.

The Collects and Naming God

I have held back until now for this, but this I believe about prayer because I am a Trinitarian. In all forms of prayer, not least in petitionary prayer, we enter in the Spirit into the presence of the Father through the Son. Every petition we make is actually the Son's own intercession for us. Hence, we pray to the Father, through the Son, in the Spirit. The Spirit, then, ushers us into the communion of Father and Son, Son with Father, as the Son and Father, who know all we want and why we are there, commune with one another.[67]

This can be a sensitive topic, for no one really wants to tell someone else what to call God when that person is praying. Should it always be "Father"? Or should we vary what we call God? Should we pray to the "Lord Jesus" or to "Jesus"? In skimming through Janet Morley's popular book of prayers called *All Desires Known*, we find addresses to God like these: Christ our Teacher, God our mother, God our lover, Holy God, Christ Jesus, Spirit of truth, Hidden God, and many others.[68] How then do we address God? Is any address biblical or most biblical or are we on our own? I want to answer those questions as we go along, but we have already seen that the Old Testament's prayers tend to be God and Lord God and LORD. The New Testament prayers shifted to Father. But let's look at how the Collect tradition has settled on the Address element of a petition.

The following addresses for God, addressed almost always to the Father regardless of which name or title is used, are found in the Collects in the *Book of Common Prayer*,[69] but what is found here is common to the entire church's use of written prayers, and they may be grouped this way:

> **Almighty**, as Almighty God (16 times), Almighty and Everlasting, or Everliving, God (10 times), Almighty and Merciful God (2 times), and Almighty Father (1 time).

> **God**, as in God (23 times), Merciful God (2 times).

> **Lord**, as in Lord (14 times), Lord God (1 time), and Lord of all power and might (1 time).

> **Father**, as in Father in Heaven or heavenly Father (2 times), Eternal Father (1 time), most loving Father (1 time), gracious Father (1 time), and Almighty Father (1 time).

Seen as a package, this is profoundly biblical. These are the terms the Bible uses in addressing God. When we address God with these terms, we confess our relationship to God. In addressing God in terms of Almighty, we announce that God is all-powerful; in addressing God as God or Lord, we publicly state that our God is the one God of all creation who rules this creation; and in addressing God as Father, we affirm our family relationship with God and with one another. It is not "my" Father but our "heavenly" Father who is Father of the heavens and the earth.

As Bible readers may quickly notice, these major names in the Collect tradition of the church span the Scriptures from Genesis to Revelation. The word "Almighty" is English for the Hebrew *El Shaddai*, God Almighty, while "Father" is the distinctive name for God used by Jesus in his own prayers and instructed by him to be used by his followers. We Christians tend to call God "Father" because of the prayer Jesus taught us, which we call "Our Father" or "The Lord's Prayer," which is still quoted by most English-speaking Christians in the King James version (Matthew 6:9–13).

Again, a momentary pause: We like to call God what we like to call God. We then need to admit that we get to choose what we will call God. We learn to pray from parents and pastors, and my father always called God "Our *heavenly* Father" with a little emphasis on "heavenly." My pastor called God "Our heavenly Father" too, and I have often wondered if my father was attached to that address because of our pastor. I sometimes hear others say, "I address God as 'The Lord God,'" while others have said to me, "I now call God 'Mother' because I don't like 'Father' and I do like 'Mother.' That's how I think of God." "OK," I reply, pausing to myself and wondering how to enter into someone's deeply personal space that that person has just revealed to me.

One doesn't in such a personal space pick a fight, but let me redirect the point to say this: the *Book of Common Prayer*'s Collects address God with four major names, and these are the major names for God in the Bible and in the church's prayer tradition. Learning to Address God in the four major names of the Collects not only instructs us but also forms us into those who see the wisdom in these addresses. But—now to answer the questions—there is no one right name or one right address. We ought to call God what seems most natural to us in the petition we are making, but we can learn from this prayer tradition about the God we are addressing. These are the most common ways the Bible itself refers to God, and it is not unwise for us to absorb these addresses for ourselves.

Now a brief word about each of the major addresses, each of which puts a name on the vastness, majesty, and glory of God—and that means no one address captures all of God but merely points us truly toward God.[70]

Almighty God

To name God in our prayers as "Almighty" affirms God's power, called "omnipotence" by theologians. "Almighty" also affirms his power to act, to save, to heal, to judge, and to make all things right. Old Testament specialists debate the meaning of *Shaddai* in Hebrew, including God of the Mountain or God of the Wilderness as in the *New Jerusalem Bible.* The NIV translates it as "Almighty." This is the translation absorbed in the entire history of the *Book of Common Prayer.* However, this term can set us off on the wrong path, so we need to think about what we are saying in addressing God as "Almighty."

We call God "Almighty" even when we know all things are not right, not just, not loving, and not wise in our world. Yet, we continue to call God "Almighty." Sometimes, even when we address God this way on a Sunday morning, doubts linger and pester us. To call God "Almighty" does not mean God is a tyrant, an emperor, or a control freak. God may be sovereign, but that sovereignty is not as sharp in profile as some like to think. Do we think our God Almighty controls life directly when children are abused by priests, when pastors grub people for every penny they can get, or when political leaders use their power to imprison falsely? Injustice is somehow within the ambit of God's Almighty-ness because God's sovereignty permits human freedom.[71] My favorite description of God as sovereign and almighty and all-powerful comes from the Old— which he calls "First"—Testament scholar, John Goldingay, and I quote him at length because every word he says matters for the one who calls God "Almighty":

> In some understandings of sovereignty, if God is sovereign,
> then many events in the world are puzzling. It's often
> impossible to see rhyme or reason behind things that happen

and things that don't happen. Because Yahweh is powerful, he is able to deliver his people (e.g., Pss 21:13 [MT 14]; 28:8), yet sometimes Yahweh lets his people be defeated, even when the defeat cannot be understood as a chastisement for their faithlessness (e.g., Ps 44). When challenged, Yahweh responds by saying. "Sorry (except that he doesn't say 'Sorry'), but the world doesn't revolve around you. You just have to live with what's happened in light of the evidence that on the whole I'm not doing too bad a job of running the world" (Job 38-41). At the same time, for people who love God, he "makes all things work together for good" (Rom 8:28). The test of God's sovereignty lies not in things that happen but in what he does with things after they happen.

Any notion, then, that Almighty means God's got everything right where God wants it and that everything will be hunky-dory is just not the way Almighty God has chosen to work. No, this Almighty-ness needs to be seen in light of the big picture, as Goldingay continues:

[The Book of] Revelation associates God's power or sovereignty with the original creation and with the new heavens and the new earth, and other scriptural assertions of God's sovereignty and power make the same connection. This association suggests a starting point for understanding God's sovereignty and power. God's sovereignty means that God alone initiated the project that brought the world into existence and that God alone will bring it to its consummation.

This is perhaps the most helpful insight I have ever learned and come to trust about our God: our Almighty God had the freedom to give us the freedom to act in freedom outside the divine will.

God's sovereignty involves a self-denying willingness for people to disobey. The all-powerful nature of God means that God can make things happen and can stop things happening; he could have stopped Eve taking the fruit from the tree, but he didn't do so. God had the capacity to send legions of angels to rescue Jesus (Mt 26:53), but he didn't do so.

Instead he let humanity do its worst, and in this way he did achieve something that he himself intended. He knew it was going to happen, he intended it to happen, and he overcame the consequences of humanity's doing its worst (Acts 2:23-24).[72]

Addressing God as "Almighty" may be the biggest claim we make. When we call God "Almighty" we stake a claim by faith that God sees, that God knows, that God is directing, and that someday all be well. To call God "Almighty" gives us confidence, conviction, and courage to believe that our God, the one true God of all creation who loves all, can judge sin, eradicate injustice and evil, and establish what is right and good. We call God "Almighty" in faith. We use this term especially when our petitions require the Almighty to act.

God

To address God as "God" or as "Lord" is to evoke the most common terms for God in the Bible. In the KJV "God" appears 3,876 times, in NRSV 4,187 times, 4,147 times in the Common English Bible, 3,808 times in the ESV, and only 3,520 times in the NIV. The differences between these are explained by the number of times translators turn an implication that "God" is present into an actual term. Other translations sometimes use "He" or "he." God is still the overwhelming subject and actor of the Bible for all the translations.

The term "God" tells a counter-cultural story in our Bible because Israel became a monotheist faith, a faith in which there truly was and is only one God. Others were polytheists, those who believed in more than one god, or henotheists, those who thought their god was superior to other gods but there were other gods. Not in Israel's faith: there is one God, and Yahweh is God's name (Genesis 14:22; Exodus 3:13–22). Everything else is a phantom God.

There is a counter-cultural story on the meaning of "God." In the Old Testament our word "God" translates *El* or its plural form *Elohim*, and as such the ancient Hebrews and Israelites borrowed a common Ancient Near East term. Various groups used various spellings of this same term *El* for their tribal God. Israel differed from surrounding nations but hijacked their term and gave it a new life in affirming but one God. Israel's defining creed is called the *Shema*: "Hear, O Israel: The LORD our God, the LORD is one" (Deuteronomy 6:4). To cut this story short: By the time of the New Testament, which was written not in Hebrew but in Greek, the term *El* translates into *Theos*. That story is behind every use of "God" in our Bibles today.

In addressing God with the word "God" we enter into a verbal confession that the God of our Lord Jesus Christ is the universe's one true cosmic God. Addressing someone in prayer as God is to bend the knee, to submit the mind, to surrender the heart, and to offer our bodies to this one God. If we do this often in our prayers we develop a rhythm of being but humans before the universe's Creator God.

What matters for the church tradition of Collects is that the Hebrew and Greek terms for God (*El, Theos*) have given way both to the English term "God" and to the church tradition that understands the Bible's teaching in Trinitarian terms. This one true God is Father, Son, and Spirit. In our routine addressing deity as "God" we develop a formation practice of knowing that our God is one-in-three and three-in-one, that our God's love for us emerges from God's own self-love: Father and Son and Spirit in an endless relationship of mutual indwelling love.

We believe in God, we confess in the Creed, "maker of heaven and earth," but we are constantly assaulted by the idolatries of our age: money, pleasure, power, reputation, glory, and possessions—to name a few. We are tempted to seek love's satisfaction in something other than relationship with God. Over and over we need to pray this term "God" to remind ourselves who is the true God and what is not.

The impact of the first two addresses—God Almighty and God—on us is that they lead us to humility and reverence and recognition that we are but a speck of dust in an ocean of time. Yet, beyond that humility we also see that our God, incredibly, includes us as the object of divine love and joy.

Lord

To call God "Lord" is similar to how the Bible uses the term "God" for God. The ESV has 6,681 uses of "Lord," the NRSV 7,225 uses, the NIV 6,466 uses; the Common English Bible uses "Lord" 7,009 times. Lord and God together swamp all other terms for God. No wonder our prayer books use God and Lord so often in addressing God!

The Hebrew term behind our translation "Lord," *Adonai*, becomes a substitute for the covenant name of God, *Yahweh*. Instead of saying "Yahweh," piety seems to have led many to say "Lord" instead. Then this Hebrew term *Adonai* becomes a Greek term, *Kyrios*, which has its own and often different cultural connections than either *Yahweh* or *El*, and this Greek term *Kyrios* becomes "Lord" in English. In the New Testament period, to call God *Kyrios* was at least to suggest that the Roman emperor, in Greek frequently called and addressed as *kyrios*, was not the world's one and only true Lord. It was also to draw on the Old Testament's two big terms for God: *Yahweh* and *Adonai*. As an address for God in prayer it has the capacity to handle about anything we want to ask for!

These terms all point to the same God, and that is why three Hebrew terms and addresses of God (*Yahweh, El, Adonai*) are brought together in the Old Testament in a summary statement in Deuteronomy 10:17, which reads: "For the LORD (*Yahweh*) your God (*El*) is God of gods and Lord (*Adonai*) of lords, the great God, mighty and awesome." These terms—God (*El*) and Yahweh/LORD/Lord (*Yahweh*)—are also brought together in the New Testament in a way that assigns one to the Father and one to the Son: "We know that 'An idol is nothing at all in the world' and that 'There is no God but one' . . . for us there is but one God (referring to Deuteronomy 6's *El*), the Father, from whom all things came and for whom we live; and there is but one Lord [referring to Deuteronomy 6's

Yahweh], Jesus Christ, through whom all things came and through whom we live" (1 Corinthians 8:4–6, NIV). Here "God" points to the Father and LORD/Yahweh points to Jesus! Yes, this kind of Trinitarian theology runs right through the Addresses of God in the Collects. Perhaps it is better to say all this is background to the Addresses we use for the word "God" or "Lord" when we pray.

A moment to pause to think through this again: It runs against the grain of the human heart to call someone else "Lord," but this is what we do in prayer. We need to utter this word with reverence and awe. One of my favorite Collects, on the Third Week after Pentecost, can perhaps remind us of a posture of reverence before the immensity of the God to whom we pray: "Grant, O Lord, that the course of this world may be peaceably governed by your providence." Our addressing God as "Lord" is a claim that our God is Lord of all creation and history, and that this Lord has a design for this world, that this Lord created this world and is shaping history toward its proper goal.

Father

While it is sometimes said neither the Old Testament nor Judaism called God "Father" and that Jesus did, so "Father" is uniquely Christian . . . the facts are not quite that simple. Isaiah 63:16 (ESV), for instance, says, "But you [Israel's God, Yahweh] are our Father."[73] The Psalms sometimes use "Father" for God or address God as "Father" (Psalms 2:7; 68:5; 89:26; 103:13). But there can be no doubt that addressing God as *Father* emerges with force in the life and teachings of Jesus and becomes the singular term for God in the writings of the apostles. When Jesus taught us to pray, he taught us to begin our prayer with "Our Father" (Matthew 6:7), and every recorded prayer of Jesus, except the cry "why have you forsaken me?," which begins with "My God, My God" (*Eli*), begins with "Father." So, addressing God as "Father" has become the distinctive address for the Christian.

"Father" blends the authority and majesty and glory and omnipotence of God and Lord with the endearment language of children and family members for the father of the family. "Father" then is the language both of family intimacy and divine authority, of love and obedience.[74] God or Lord enters the home to become "Father."

However, something must also be said about the term "Father." It is a sad reality that for many their earthly father has been abusive, sometimes sexually and other times verbally and emotionally and psychologically. Consequently, many are troubled by this common and paradigmatic Christian term of address for God. Some cannot pray this term and will either go silent or will substitute another term, perhaps Lord or God or even Mother. One can suggest in response that calling God "Father" can become for some a way of subverting abusive earthly fathers and replacing that abusive father with a loving, caring, protecting, and safe Father. What follows flows from that conviction, but only for those who share that conviction.

We address God as "Father" weekly and daily in the Lord's Prayer as well. In addition, many of us were taught to address God as Father in our prayers. Hence, we constantly participate in this term, making it particularly susceptible to neglect if not casual meaninglessness. To repeat, our casualness may also be a source of pain for those who have been abused by a father. Yet, "Father" is also an address full of wonderful expectations. On the first of January the Collect for the day called "Holy Name," we pray, "Eternal Father, you gave to your incarnate Son the holy name of Jesus to be the sign of our salvation." While on the First Sunday after the Epiphany, on the day we focus on the baptism of Jesus, we pray, "Father in heaven, who at the baptism of Jesus in the River Jordan proclaimed him your beloved Son and anointed him with the Holy Spirit." One more "Father" Collect: on the Eighth Sunday after the Epiphany we pray "Most loving Father," an intimacy not often found in Collects, but the elements of Ask God and Expect God explain why we work back to an address of God that fits:

Preserve us from faithless fears and worldly anxieties, *that no clouds of this mortal life may hide from us the light of that love which is immortal, and which you have manifested to us in your Son Jesus Christ our Lord.*

To address God as Father, and to do so constantly, is to form us into God's children and to form us into siblings with one another. We need over and over to Address God as Father because we are in need of a stronger conviction that we are God's children and we need to live more often with one another as siblings. We are full of rivalries in the church, and while we are uttering prayers with the word "Father" as our term of address, we are split and divided into denominations and churches that refuse to countenance one another. Perhaps the Address "Father" can become a source of union among Christians of all stripes.

Once again, there is no need to think we are to use terms of address for God that are "approved" or used in the church's Collect tradition. God hears our prayers regardless of which terms we choose or prefer. Yet, perhaps we could give more attention to the Address of our prayers by pondering the evocations and theology that flow directly from calling God terms like Almighty, God, Lord, and Father.

10

ACCESS GOD, THROUGH CHRIST, IN THE SPIRIT

The New Testament's theological contribution to the pattern of petitionary prayer is that we have Access to God through Christ, and we are empowered to do this in the Spirit of God. Access through Christ is stated in Hebrews 4:14–16:

> Since, then, we have a great high priest who has passed
> through the heavens, Jesus, the Son of God, let us hold fast to
> our confession. For we do not have a high priest who is unable
> to sympathize with our weaknesses, but we have one who in
> every respect has been tested as we are, yet without sin. Let us
> therefore approach the throne of grace with boldness, so that
> we may receive mercy and find grace to help in time of need.

The Collect tradition, which again is but the crystallization of the biblical and church's pattern for petitions, reminds us of the means of our access to God, and hence in some studies this is called the Plea or Pleading.[75] I have categorized this element "Access God" because it nearly always says "through."

To make this clear: the New Testament's prayers do not always finish with "Through Christ," though Romans 16:27 does ("through Jesus Christ"), and "Amen" itself is quite uncommon (see Romans 9:5; 11:36; 15:33; 16:27). 2 Corinthians 1:20, speaking of Christ, says, "For this reason it is through him that we say the 'Amen,' to the glory of God."[76] Yet, the theology of the New Testament is that we Access God through Christ and in the Spirit.

This is our means of access, and it is given to us by God's grace in Christ. Here is the most common Grace that finishes a Collect:

> Through Jesus Christ your Son our Lord, who lives and
> reigns with you and the Holy Spirit, one God, now and for
> ever. *Amen.*

Our access to God—giving us confidence to Address God in the terms we use and to Remind God of who God is and what God has done in the past, giving us confidence as well to Ask God and follow the petition with the Expect God to answer element—is "through Jesus Christ your Son our Lord." This means the prayer is addressed to the Father or to our Trinitarian God through the Son in the power of the Spirit. We are privileged to offer these petitions solely through the merits of Jesus Christ who, in his life, death, burial, and resurrection has provided redemption for us and access to the God of all creation.

This Jesus not only died and was raised but is "now and for ever" active for us—we call this the "session" of Christ—as our great high priest and as our ruling king. He sits at the right of the Father with the Holy Spirit—and we affirm our Trinitarian faith that Father and Son and Spirit are "one God."

In the world of Jesus the person praying did not close off his or her prayer by saying "Amen," because they knew the meaning of the term. It is Aramaic for "so be it" or even "I agree." It was a term used by those who heard the prayer and agreed with it, and it was how they participated. In our day the person praying says "Amen," and in the public worship by those using these petitions we all say "Amen," and that is why it is in italics.

11

PRAYING THE PATTERN
A Summary

I want now to summarize once again the major elements in learning to compose our own petitions in a way that is consistent with the biblical and church pattern for petitionary prayers. Those elements are these:

Address God
Remind God
Ask God
Expect God
Access God Through Christ, In the Spirit

Though the pattern does begin with addressing God and reminding God, and that is where we always begin our prayers, the genius of the Bible's own pattern for our petitions is that they are asking God for something. They request something of God, and that means the Collects, which crystallize the biblical pattern, are shaped by one and only one thing that matters: what the praying person desires. So in this final chapter we want to walk through the practice of praying according to this pattern one more time.

Begin with Your Petition

The one praying in the Collect tradition prays from the middle, then goes backward and then forward. The petitioner constructs the Address God and Remind God elements on the basis of the Ask God element. The petition's composition order is then different from the logical order. The Address and Remind God do lead to the Ask God element, to be sure, but they were constructed because of the nature of the petition. Another way of saying this is that this pattern for petitionary prayer is an organic whole with each element cooperating with the others.

Make Your Petition Specific

What is it that you really want from God? That is the question that launches a genuine petition. I encourage you to think of something specific—"our church needs a new building or an extension" or "my daughter's success and healing in a surgery" or "I want a better job where I can flourish more"—and one could list the many desires of your heart. But make it specific. Don't hold back. The church's petition tradition has never been bashful or abstract. It is bold and direct.

Deliberate for the Remind God Element

When I have prayed according to this pattern, which I have done thousands of times in my life, it is the Remind God that most occupies my attention and musings. When one prays for healing, one can deliberate on passages about healing, perhaps address God as "Father," and speak this truth about God from Exodus 15:26: "you are the One who heals." Exodus says, "I am the LORD who heals you." Or, based on Acts 9:34's claim that "Jesus Christ heals you," we might pray, "Father, who in your Son sent to us our healer." Or, more fluidly, "Father, who has healed Naaman the Syrian, Hezekiah the king, Mary of Magdala, and the Centurion's servant." Or perhaps "Father, you have healed often in the past."

It does not require one to be a theologian to deliberate on truths about God, but it does require some thinking to connect the petition we have to truths about God. We are thinking theologically when we do this, and we are appealing—as Solomon did in his prayers, as did David and the prophets, as did Jesus in the Lord's Prayer, and as did Paul in his opening prayers to his letters—to God on the basis of who God is and what God does. It is not manipulative to say to God: "Father, you are gracious, so be gracious to me." It is more anchored in our deepest theology to say that than to barge in with "Give me what I want!" Asking God to be consistent with God's own God-ness is hardly manipulative. It is in fact affirming God's God-ness in God's presence.

So, let's agree that our prayer is for someone's healing and we address God as "Father" and we appeal to these simple truths: "You are the one who heals, you are the one who has healed, and your Son was sent as our healer."

Consider the Best Address

The four major addresses of the Bible and the church prayer tradition—Almighty, God, Lord, and Father, and variants of each—may be the most common terms of address to God in prayer both in the Bible and in the church tradition, but they are not the only ones. The Bible's pattern is:

To the Father,

through the Son,

in the Spirit.

Furthermore, it is not possible (theologically speaking) to have the Grace of this prayer—"through Jesus Christ our Lord"—if we are addressing Jesus in the prayer. Yet, while I affirm this way of prayer I am aware that many, because of their Trinitarian theology, will address some prayers to the Son and others to the Spirit along with most to the Father. Stephen, the martyr, had a final prayer just before being killed: "Lord Jesus, receive my spirit" (Acts 7:59). Ananias, too, prayed to the "Lord" when it is clear he was in dialogue with Jesus about what to do with the problem called Saul (Acts 9:13–17).

Let's say you are praying for a better job. You might ponder God as Almighty because something big has to happen for a job to open that most suits your gifts. Or, you might want to begin with God, who is in and over all, or the Lord, who rules the universe. Or, you might begin with Father because you are thinking more in terms of God's love being directed toward you in a new job.

There are other terms for address, however. One could address God as the "Lord of hosts" or, as John Goldingay's translation has it, "Yahweh of Armies."[77] Or as God Most High, or even The Jealous One, for Exodus 34:14 (NIV) says, "Do not worship any other god, for the LORD, whose name is Jealous, is a jealous God." One might anchor a petition in The Jealous One when one desires for God to be glorified in the midst of God's being dishonored.

Express What You Expect When God Answers the Petition

The "that" clause of the Collect can check our selfishness at the door. In constructing the Ask God element we need to ask ourselves, "Why am I asking this?" or "What will happen if God answers this prayer?" It's oh-so right to say, "So God will be glorified," but the prayers of the church instruct us to think a little more thoughtfully about our expectations. We will here want to push the petition into the hopes and dreams and imaginings: for example, so the mission in our local church might flourish, or so the children of the sick person will have a mother, or so the family's income will not be jeopardized.

So we ask. We put our petition into words and attach to that petition the Expect God to answer element.

"Father, you are the one who heals, you are the one who has healed, and your Son was sent as our healer; Grant that *N.* be healed from this sickness, *that* she can return to her work and flourish in the ministry to which you have called her, for which there is no replacement and which is greatly needed." This of course could be adapted and adjusted in many ways. Our intention here is but to illustrate how a petition can lead to a goal that takes our prayer to the next level.

Recognize Your Sole Access is through Christ and In the Spirit

Remember, petitions are petitions. We are asking God for something specific. We Address God and we Remind God with truths that are consistent with the petition and we shape the petition, so it fits into the larger plans of God. But we can only present our petition to God on the basis of the grace and merits of what Jesus Christ, our Lord, has done for us. He has rescued us from sin and presented us as worthy in the presence of God on the basis of his work and ministry. We are prompted by God's Spirit to ask such things of God. It is solely by Christ's work that we enter into the Father's presence. Hence, we finish our prayer with this:

> Through Jesus Christ your Son our Lord, who lives and reigns with you and the Holy Spirit, one God, now and for ever. *Amen.*

So our new Collect, and you will want to practice writing your own Collects, is this:

> *Father*, <u>you are the one who heals, you are the one who has healed, and your Son was sent as our healer;</u> **Grant that *N.* be healed from this sickness,** *that she can return to her work and flourish in the ministry to which you have called her, for which there is no replacement and which is greatly needed.* Through Jesus Christ your Son our Lord, who lives and reigns with you and the Holy Spirit, one God, now and for ever. *Amen.*

APPENDIX

GETTING THE MOST OUT OF PUBLIC PRAYER

R egardless of how one prays, praying is the participation of the whole person and body. The mind, spirit, soul, heart, conscience, tongue, eyes, hands, legs . . . the whole body is involved. When it comes to Collects, and this Appendix is especially suitable for Anglicans or those who use Collects, we not only pray like that but we pray together—all of us—as an assembly of Christians. The pastor leads us and we pray along, and then we take these prayers into our homes to pray personally and privately. There are four dimensions of learning that occur as we learn to pray with the church's tradition of petitionary prayer:

> participation,
> expectation,
> formation,
> and instruction.

A brief word about each as they help each of us learn to pray.

Participation

Anglican author L .E. H. Stephens-Hodge points his finger at a reality many of us know by experience with those who question the appropriateness of using written prayers: "In Free Church worship, where extempore prayer is normal, the responsibility for making the seasons of prayer relevant largely rests upon the minister; where a liturgy is used, as in our own Church, it rests equally upon every member of the congregation."[78] For many a prayer is either one's own private extemporary prayer or it is not prayer at all. I contend the church Collect prayers lead us into participation.

We come to church not just to sit and watch and listen and get something and go home and eat. We come to participate. We stand and sit and stand and sit and stand and sit, then we walk around among one another and offer the greeting of peace—"The peace of Christ be with you"—and then we sit and walk forward and take the Eucharist and sit down and stand and then we leave or, in our case, have some coffee and treats and chatter with one another about life.

Praying a Collect involves two kinds of participation: First, the Collect of the Week is prayed aloud by our pastor as we read and listen along and say it to ourselves and then say a hearty "Amen!" in affirmation of the Collect. Second, the Collect is also called the Collect for the Week because we are encouraged to pray that same Collect during the week as we follow along the in the *Book of Common Prayer*'s daily Bible readings and prayers for Morning and Evening Prayer. Hence, we participate both by being led into the Collect and by saying it ourselves. In this book I emphasize our *participation* in the Collect, and by that I mean we pray it in both listening to it and by verbally saying it ourselves.

More can be said: the pastor who prays the Collect leads us and represents us and models to us what to pray and how to pray. Any pastor who offers a pastoral prayer for a congregation performs a priestly act in taking to God our concerns. Any Christian who prays for another— who expresses a petition—also acts in a priestly manner with others. Yet, when others pray, we participate as well—by listening, reading, and praying ourselves.

When we pray the Collects, we join Anglicans and Methodists and Presbyterians and Lutherans and other liturgical traditions who are praying these or similar Collects.[79] There is a wave of prayer across the globe all day long as various pastors, priests, and other Christians are praying their petitions. We *all* participate in the Collect. In the Collect tradition, whether we say them on Sunday or on Thursday alone, we embody our belief in the communion of the saints.

Expectation

The expectation dimension is especially relevant to our Sunday worship services, whichever one's tradition (Anglican, Methodist, Presbyterian, Roman Catholic). Practice in gathered worship informs us that the Collect often anticipates what will occur during the worship service, especially the Scripture readings.[80] So on the Sunday called Epiphany, or the appearing and manifestation of Christ to the world, we petition God in this way:

> O God, by the leading of a star you manifested your only
> Son to the peoples of the earth: Lead us, who know you now
> by faith, to your presence, where we may see your glory
> face to face; through Jesus Christ our Lord, who lives and
> reigns with you and the Holy Spirit, one God, now and for
> ever. Amen.

This Collect leads us to expect a reading about the "leading of a star" and Jesus appearing to "the peoples of the earth." These both occur in the Gospel reading about the magi, Matthew 2:1–12. The point of the magi story is that magi are foreigners, that is, gentiles, who are the first to offer gifts to Israel's Messiah. The promises to Abraham to bless all nations is thus fulfilled in this text we read for Epiphany. The Collect puts it all into prayer and leads us to expect this important theme in our faith: that God's grace is revealed in Christ for all.

There's more to this expectation in our corporate worship: these special Sunday prayers also lead us to expect the great events of the church calendar. Epiphany will give way to Lent, and Lent will give way to Holy Week and Easter, and Easter to Pentecost and Pentecost to Trinity Sunday and the weeks after Pentecost until the next Advent. Each of these seasons in the church focuses on the life and teachings and mission of Jesus, and so we are led by our Collects to expect to hear more and more about Jesus.

I have learned in saying the Sunday Collect in personal devotion throughout the week that the dimension of expectation is intensified, both in more Scripture readings for the weekdays and also in repeating the petition each day the themes of the year are drilled deeper into my heart.

Formation

Much has been said in the last generation when discussing ethics, and this discussion focuses on (1) *practices* (2) *forming* us into (3) *a people of virtue*. Some have said that we are not even Christian until we are being formed in the context of a community, and there's not a little truth in that rhetorical exaggeration. Christian formation then is not just about me and God, about my personal spiritual formation disciplines (solitude, prayer, fasting, etc.), but about learning to live as Christians with one another. The Collects are part of our formation as a people, and they are but one part of the formative power of prayer books like the *Book of Common Prayer*.[81]

Let's break this down a little more. There is an undeniable formational power in our habits or practices, what some today call *habitus*. All of the church's Collects have the potential, when used as intended, to form us. Indeed, one might say they are always forming us. Perhaps we can think of the gathered church as a stage filled with humans called to perform the gospel with one another. "The church," Reformed theologian Kevin Vanhoozer observes, "is a company of players gathered together to stage scenes of the kingdom of God for the sake of a watching world. The direction of doctrine thus enables us, as individuals and as a church, to render the gospel public by leading lives in creative imitation of Christ."[82] When we play our part, guided by the Scriptures, we learn also how better and best to play our part.

Charles Hefling said much the same in describing the *Book of Common Prayer*'s use: "Like a dramatic script, it prescribes what is to happen by describing it in advance. Different speeches are assigned to different characters, who play different roles, individually or collectively, by speaking lines that the book prints in full, and following 'rubrics', the stage directions, as it were, that specify what is to be done and explain how the various components of the liturgy are ordered."[83] The word "play" is the issue here: we can play at play or genuinely perform/play our part.

Think of this play as a circle: *You (or We)* stand at the bottom and say the *Prayers*, which lead up the circle to the left to the top where you enter the world of your common *Practices*, and these *Practices* turn you into a character-forming *Habitus* on the right that leads in such a way that the *Habitus* impacts *You* toward deeper formation. Entering into this circle we can become formed by the circle. Our practices form us. We might call this the Circle of Collect Formation:

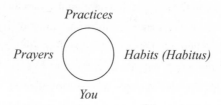

Practices

Prayers   *Habits (Habitus)*

You

A warning, one well worth hearing more than once. Lauren Winner wisely contends that our spiritual habits are neither neutral nor always formationally virtuous. She contends in some contexts those practices meant for good can become nasty deformations instead of positive formations or reformations. Why and How? Sin and Flesh, to get to the point. Winner puts it this way,

> Sin is what's ushered in by the Fall and produces all this
> damage. That is, the word "sin" denotes habits, actions,
> and proclivities of human beings (and other creatures with
> agency, such as angels and perhaps certain other nonhuman
> primates) that draw what God created away from God and
> that unleash damage into the world.

If this is the world in which we live, our practices can become sullied with Sin and Flesh, and Winner continues with precise analytical language: "Things become deformed by sin in ways that are proper to the thing being deformed, and when those deformations have consequences, you cannot separate the consequences from the deformed thing itself, because it belongs to the thing potentially to have those very consequences."[84] This can sound a little abstract, but Winner explores Eucharist, which at times became the opportunity for some Christians to *deform* the very meal of Jesus into murdering Jews for murdering Jesus! How, one might ask, can the glorious practice of

Eucharist turn those receiving into murderers?! Then she looks at prayer in the hands of slave owners which, in a grand act of pious deformation, becomes "commandeering petitionary prayer"[85] or "the wagon with which one keeps circling around a misbegotten object of desire,"[86] including damnation of one's slaves while purportedly praying for their redemption! And, finally, she turns to baptism, which can become a celebration of social status and economic privilege divorced physically from church and community, which shows again the power of a habit or spiritual practice to become deformational.

There you go: practices such as Eucharist, prayer, and baptism become the opposite of what they are designed by God to be. Instead of becoming agents of grace they become agents of murder, condescension, and exclusivism. Practices are not automatic. Practices without the good graces of God can become agents of sin, flesh, world, and evil.

Praying the Collects, which is one of the foci of this book, can become deformed. I suggest in at least two ways: when they are little more than mouthing the words, or when they become sanctified piety—that is, when they become for us tools by which we assess whether someone can pray well or not, tools with which compare ourselves to others who know not how to pray as we ought! The sinner who said "Be merciful" is as eloquent as any Collect ever composed!

Our larger point is this: praying the church's petitionary prayer tradition, the Collects, can be spiritually formative (or deformative) for us. If we participate intentionally, if we listen to the words of the Collect and through them expect the redemptive work of God, these composed prayers can become formational for us.

Instruction

The focus of this book is on the formational and instructional value of the Bible's and church's pattern of petition. We can learn to pray by praying the Collects. We learn to pray most by praying, and praying over time yields wisdom about prayer. But the Collects can launch a new career of prayer, they can suddenly act in ways that are healing, and they can instruct us. Anglicans believe our theology is found in prayers, and our prayers put into words our theology. If we give careful attention to our Collects, we will discover the span of Christian theology and gospel faith.

Liturgy is pedagogy, as is often said. Which is to say, our Collects instruct us in prayer and theology. Sometimes we pray at length, like Psalm 78, but other times we pray succinctly, quickly, and directly. Jesus once taught us to pray with brevity. In the Sermon on the Mount Jesus a few times countered his way of life with how others did things. "When you pray," he said, "do not be like the hypocrites, for they love to pray standing in the synagogues and on the street corners to be seen by others." Jesus instructed his followers to pray in private instead of praying ostentatiously like the "hypocrites," because God can see into the secret places (Matthew 6:5–6, NIV). Now comes the brevity part when he counters the way "pagans" pray: "And when you pray, do not keep on babbling like pagans, for they think they will be heard because of their many words. Do not be like them, for your Father knows what you need before you ask him" (6:7–8, NIV).

Jesus' instruction, which we call the Lord's Prayer, *illustrates succinct, brief, and to-the-point prayers*. Jesus followed that "do not" with this "do": "This, then, is how you should pray." Again, the Lord's Prayer is a brilliant masterpiece of concision and brevity, and it instructs us that at times we need to get to the point and lay our petitions before God in the clearest and simplest of words. One of the great instructions by those who teach us to write is to write simply, and I recall reading a book that said, at least this is how I remember it, *What you say in two sentences can be said in one*. Two of William Zinsser's favorite words in that book are "simplicity" and "clutter."[87] The Lord's Prayer has simplicity and avoids clutter. The Collects express this very teaching of Jesus: let your words be few, speak your mind to Our Father, God is listening.

The Requirements for Formation

A final word, one that for me is vital and one that is not emphasized enough by those who discuss habits and practices as formational. I draw our attention again to the *de*-formational power of praying the Collects. The danger of the Collects is their practice, their habitual use, the saying of the words over and over without reflection, without intention, and without praying for God's grace to be at work. So, we need to be aware of this danger of their capacity to be deformations.

For the Collects to form us we need the following three realities: no formation occurs without *God's grace*, and the Collects will reveal the constant request of "Grant" that is nothing less than a request for God's grace. Second, we need the *Holy Spirit*, without whom we will never be changed into the likeness of Christ. 2 Corinthians 3:17–18 (NIV) states this beautifully: "Now the Lord is the Spirit, and where the Spirit of the Lord is, there is freedom. And we all, who with unveiled faces contemplate the Lord's glory, are being transformed into his image with ever-increasing glory, which comes from the Lord, who is the Spirit." The Spirit, not our willpower or discipline, converts us from bondage to sin and evil into freedom in Christ. What I label the "Access" of the Collects brings the Spirit into almost every Collect: "through Jesus Christ our Lord, to whom, with you and the Holy Spirit, be honor and glory, now and for ever."

Humans, however, need to respond, and the fundamental response in the Bible is *faith that becomes love or love that becomes faith*. We are to read the Collect and say the Collect in faith, loving God, or loving God in faith. This is not magic. The Collects don't do their work by themselves, and neither can we manufacture formation. We need God's grace and the attending Holy Spirit, and we need to be open in faith to the Spirit's work in God's grace. I give space again to Stephens-Hodge, who reminds us of the need for grace in the expression "ardour" when he says, "Familiar words, known in advance, are made incandescent, as it were, by the ardour of individual devotion, and become the vehicle of contemporary needs and desires."[88]

There are then four dimensions of praying the Collects: participation, expectation, formation, and instruction—all shaped toward our transformation by God's grace, the attending power of the Holy Spirit as we learn to love God in faith. Prior to praying a Collect, we need to pause in silence to invoke God's grace and the Spirit as we trust God to speak to us as we speak to God in that Collect.

AFTER WORDS

I did not plan a series of books on Anglican practices and theology when I wrote *It Takes a Church to Baptize*. That book came about because I had written a long excursus on infant baptism for a commentary on Colossians (with Wm. B. Eerdmans). That excursus's size necessitated thinking of another kind of publication, and so the book for Baker on baptism came to be. A few friends have asked me if, to complement the book on baptism, whether I might do a book on Eucharist, and I responded that I wanted first to do a small study about the Collects as a paradigm for improving both private and public prayer. So this book.

Thanks to Fr. Arnie Klukas for recommendations on resources about the Collects and the *BCP*, and to my pastor, Jay Greener, for occasional comments and for a few observations one evening that sent me to make a comprehensive revision. Thanks, too, for his gift to lead us in praying the Collects in such a manner that I sometimes wonder if we haven't all said them aloud. I am grateful to Charles Hefling for answering a few of my questions. Fred Long at Asbury Seminary made a suggestion that greatly improved the book, and I thank him for it. Thanks, too, to Justin Gill, my graduate assistant, for acquiring through our library systems items to read for this book.

Kris and I offer a special thanks to Nikolette and Marin, Despina and Maria, our exuberant and gracious hosts at Hotel Grotta on Naxos (Greece), where the first draft of this book took shape. From our hotel room balcony we looked down onto the Aegean and could see both some ruins of the temple to Apollo as well as a magnificent Greek Orthodox Church (Metropolis of Naxos, dedicated to Zoodochos Pigi), where we had our first experience of a Greek Easter midnight service. The word "raucous" would be appropriate for the Easter service, but tranquility is the word for our hotel. Hotel Grotta kindly provided me a desk in our room and, with our doors open and the Aegean breezing through the room, what was raucous became two weeks of reverent study of the wonderful prayers in *The Book of Common Prayer*, a book once described by Rowan Williams as "a doctrinal and devotional climate."[89] The Aegean climate made it more doctrinal and devotional.

NOTES

1 Herbert Lockyer, *All the Prayers of the Bible* (Grand Rapids, MI: Zondervan, 1959), 5.

2 John Baillie, *A Diary of Private Prayer* (New York: Simon & Schuster/Firestone, 1996), 101.

3 All citations from the Bible are from the NRSV unless noted otherwise. The NRSV, with more clear echoes of the KJV, has tones of reverence for prayers not found in more recent translations.

4 Notice, too, Exodus 3–4 where Moses negotiates with God about his calling to deliver the children of Israel. Also: Exodus 32:31–32.

5 See, too, Exodus 32:11–14 for another prayer in which Moses reminds God.

6 J. Charlesworth, ed., *The Old Testament Pseudepigrapha*, trans. by C. Burchard (New York: Doubleday, 1985).

7 Emil Schurer, *The History of the Jewish People in the Age of Jesus Christ*, ed. G. Vermes et al., 2nd Revised edition (T & T Clark, 1987), 2.456, 457.

8 The Episcopal Church, *The Book of Common Prayer* (New York: Oxford University Press, 1990), 355.

9 Bridget Nichols, ed., *The Collect in the Churches of the Reformation*, SCM Studies in Worship and Liturgy (London: SCM, 2010), 1. For her succinct study of the translation and elegance and style of the Collects, see "The Collect in English: Vernacular Beginnings," in Nichols, 9–27.

10 Charles Hefling and Cynthia Shattuck, eds., *The Oxford Guide to The Book of Common Prayer: A Worldwide Survey* (Oxford: Oxford University Press, 2006), 567.

11 See Charles Lett Feltoe, "Collects," in *The Prayer Book Dictionary*, ed. George Harford and Morley Stevenson (London: Pitman and Sons, 1912), 211. J. Neil Alexander writes the following on the origin of the Collects:

> Collects are brief prayers unique to western liturgical tradition. In the Prayer Book tradition, approximately two-thirds of the collects are English translations of pre-Reformation Latin collects. The remainder are either new compositions or represent the considerable reworking of earlier materials.
>
> Through much of liturgical history, the use of a collect signals the completion of a larger liturgical unit. The presider 'collected' both the people and their prayers so that the next part of the liturgy could proceed. In the Prayer Book tradition up through the 1662 book, only the collect before the readings was retained and it became, in common practice, the collect 'of the day', a practice that has its roots in the liturgical revisions of continental Lutheranism. This shift in the use of the collect, from the terminating prayer of a liturgical action to a short, variable prayer standing alone, sets the stage for the proliferation of collects for every conceivable need or occasion.

His chapter is called "The Shape of the Classical Book of Common Prayer," in Hefling and Shattuck, *Oxford Guide to BCP*, 71.

12 A description of this criticism can be seen in the excellent study of prayer among Baptists, which in some contexts uses written prayers like the Collects, by Chris Ellis, "Written Prayers in an Oral Context: Transitions in British Baptist Worship," in Nichols, *The Collect*, 139–56.

13 For a longer defense, see Scot McKnight, *Praying with the Church: Following Jesus Daily, Hourly, Today* (Brewster, MA: Paraclete Press, 2006), 23–66.

14 Robert Elmer, ed., *Piercing Heaven: Prayers of the Puritans* (Bellingham, WA: Lexham Press, 2019).

15 C. S. Lewis, *Letters to Malcolm, Chiefly on Prayer* (San Francisco: HarperOne, 2017).

16 Also called *Amidah* or *Shemeneh Esreh* or "Eighteen Benedictions."

17 Schurer, *History of the Jewish People*, 2.456, 457.

18 Donald Gray, "Cranmer and the Collects," in *The Oxford Handbook of English Literature and Theology*, ed. Andrew Hass, David Jasper, and Elisabeth Jay (New York: Oxford University Press, 2007), 562.

19 L. E. H. Stephens-Hodge, *The Collects*, The Prayer Book Commentaries (London: Hodder & Stoughton, 1964), 15–17. An older version saw three elements (invocation = our 1 and 2; the petition = our 3 and 4; and the pleading of Christ's name, or ascription); see Feltoe, "Collects," 211.

20 Marion J. Hatchett, *Commentary on the American Prayer Book* (New York: HarperOne, 1995), 164.

21 Alan Jacobs, *The "Book of Common Prayer": A Biography*, Lives of Great Religious Books (Princeton and Oxford: Princeton University Press, 2013), 32.

22 The Episcopal Church, *BCP*, 355.

23 Aidan Kavanagh, *On Liturgical Theology* (Collegeville, MN: Pueblo/Liturgical Press, 1992), 48.

24 Stephens-Hodge, *The Collects*, 24–25. I have edited his words to make them more inclusive.

25 These two prayers are found in The Episcopal Church, *Book of Common Prayer*, 135, 137.

26 Of the many prayer books I mention these: 1) William Bright, *Ancient Collects and Other Prayers: Selected for Devotional Use from Various Rituals, with an Appendix, on the Collects in the Prayer-Book*, 3d ed. (Oxford: J.H. & Jas. Parker, 1864). 2) John Baillie, *A Diary of Private Prayer* (note 2). 3) L. E. H. Stephens-Hodge, *The Collects* (note 19). 4) Marion J. Hatchett, *Commentary on the American Prayer Book* (note 20). 5) Walter Brueggemann, *Awed to Heaven, Rooted in Earth* (note 53).

27 Miroslav Volf and Matthew Croasmun, *For the Life of the World: Theology That Makes a Difference* (Grand Rapids, MI: Brazos, 2019), 132.

28 Janet Morley, *All Desires Known: Third Edition*, 3d ed. (Harrisburg, PA: Morehouse, 2006), 86.

29 For a succinct analysis of the history of this prayer and who uses it and where it is used in public worship, see Hatchett, *Commentary on the American Prayer Book*, 381–82.

30 The Episcopal Church, *Book of Common Prayer*, 337.

31 The Episcopal Church, *Book of Common Prayer*, 364–65.

32 https://www.cnbc.com/2019/07/03/advice-from-90-year-olds-how-to-live-a-long-happy-and-regret-free-life.html

33 Northumbria Community, *Celtic Daily Prayer* (San Francisco, CA: HarperSanFrancisco, 2002), 18–19.

34 The Episcopal Church, *Book of Common Prayer*, 360.

35 Frank Colquhoun, ed., *Parish Prayers* (London: Hodder & Stoughton, 2000), 219–20.

36 Morley, *All Desires Known*, 7.

37 John Goldingay, *The First Testament: A New Translation* (Downers Grove, IL: InterVarsity Press, 2018), 923.

38 Goldingay, *The First Testament*, 923.

39 Three very good studies are Matthew W. Bates, *Salvation by Allegiance Alone: Rethinking Faith, Works, and the Gospel of Jesus the King* (Grand Rapids, MI: Baker Academic, 2017); Bates, *Gospel Allegiance* (Grand Rapids, MI: Brazos Press, 2019); Nijay K. Gupta, *Paul and the Language of Faith* (Grand Rapids, MI: Wm. B. Eerdmans, 2019).

40 During the weeks of the Season after Pentecost (or after Trinity Sunday), or during what is called by some "Ordinary Time," the Collects and readings are listed in the *Book of Common Prayer* as "Proper" with a number (e.g., Proper 23). The week itself is not a "Proper" Week though that is what one might think in looking at the *Book of Common Prayer*. Thus, for "The Season after Pentecost" for the Sunday closest to May 11 the *Book of Common Prayer* says "Proper 1" in bold letters. That is not the name of the Week but instead the "Proper" or appropriate readings and Collects to be used on the week designated for it. In *It Takes a Church to Pray* I will use the number with the term "Proper" with its number to designate the Collects in the Season after Pentecost. I do this because not every "Proper" is used every year. It is 2019 as I write this paragraph. Trinity Sunday is June 16 so the first week of the Season after Pentecost to which a "Proper" is assigned is in June 23. The Proper for that day though is "Proper 7" because "Ordinary Time" was reduced to accommodate a longer Eastertide! This can be confusing to figure out, but if one just goes to the *Book of Common Prayer* or to lectionarypage.net one will be on sure ground: they tell us which Proper is appropriate for that calendar date.

41 For this, see Scot McKnight, "Saints Re-Formed: The Extension and Expansion of *Hagios* in Paul," in *One God, One People, One Future: Essays in Honour of N.T. Wright*, ed. John A. Dunne and Eric Lewellen (Minneapolis, MN: Fortress Press, 2018), 211–31.

42 By William Temple; from Colquhoun, *Parish Prayers*, 385.

43 I work this out in a few books; see the most recent in Scot McKnight, *Pastor Paul: Nurturing a Culture of Christoformity in the Church*, Theological Explorations for the Church Catholic (Grand Rapids, MI: Brazos, 2019), 41–46.

44 Northumbria Community, *Celtic Daily Prayer*, 19.

45 Morley, *All Desires Known*, 24.
46 Samuel Wells and Abigail Kocher, *Shaping the Prayers of the People: The Art of Intercession* (Grand Rapids, MI: Wm. B. Eerdmans, 2014), 20.
47 A variant form from Prosper of Aquitaine is *Legem credendi lex statuat supplicandi*, which in translation is "let the rule for petition determine the rule for belief." This is the finest description or statement I know for the Collects.
48 Strong explanations of this can be found in Kavanagh, *On Liturgical Theology*; Alexander Schmemann, *For the Life of the World: Sacraments and Orthodoxy* (Crestwood, NY: St Vladimir's Seminary Press, 2000). Kavanagh throughout his book calls liturgy "primary" theology and our theological ideas "secondary." At times he overstates his claims, making one think the origins of the church are in a liturgical service, but in Kavanagh I've found someone who gripes about systematics more than I do!
49 St Nikodimos of the Holy Mountain and St Makarios of Corinth, eds., *The Philokalia: The Complete Text*, trans. G. E. H. Palmer, Philip Sherrard, and Kallistos Ware, vol. 1 (London: Faber and Faber, 1983), 1.62.
50 Kavanagh, *On Liturgical Theology*, 100.
51 Hefling and Shattuck, *Oxford Guide to the Book of Common Prayer*, 3. Cited as is found in the text.
52 John M. G. Barclay, *Paul and the Gift* (Grand Rapids, MI: Wm. B. Eerdmans, 2015), 185. He does not use "theme" but "perfections." His dictionary-type definition of grace, from p. 575, is worth recording here:

"Gift" denotes the sphere of voluntary, personal relations, characterized by goodwill in the giving of benefit or favor, and eliciting some form of reciprocal return that is both voluntary and necessary for the continuation of the relationship. In accord with the anthropology of gift, its scope includes various forms of kindness, favor, generosity, or compassion enacted in diverse services and benefits, with the expectation of some reciprocating gratitude or counter-gift. Ancient languages articulate this field of relations in a rich variety of terms, which often overlap in meaning but may also contain subtly different connotations.

53 Walter Brueggemann, *Awed to Heaven, Rooted in Earth* (Philadelphia: Fortress, 2002), 142–43.
54 http://www.rachelbarrentine.com/blog/2016/10/24/a-prayer-to-remember-the-goodness-of-god
55 Michael J. Gorman, *Cruciformity: Paul's Narrative Spirituality of the Cross* (Grand Rapids, MI: Wm. B. Eerdmans, 2001); Michael J. Gorman, *Inhabiting the Cruciform God: Kenosis, Justification, and Theosis in Paul's Narrative Soteriology* (Grand Rapids, MI: Wm. B. Eerdmans, 2009); Michael J. Gorman, *Becoming the Gospel: Paul, Participation, and Mission* (Grand Rapids, MI: Wm. B. Eerdmans, 2015).
56 McKnight, *Pastor Paul*.
57 C. Frederick Barbee and Paul F.M. Zahl, *The Collects of Thomas Cranmer* (Grand Rapids, MI: Wm. B. Eerdmans, 1999).
58 Brueggemann, *Awed to Heaven, Rooted in Earth*, 168.
59 Wells and Kocher, *Shaping the Prayers of the People: The Art of Intercession*, 14.
60 Wells and Kocher, *Shaping the Prayers*, 36.
61 That is, neglecting the Collects for special days like Holy Days or various occasions like the anniversary of a church's dedication.
62 Northumbria Community, *Celtic Daily Prayer*, 39.
63 Northumbria Community, *Celtic Daily Prayer*, 42.
64 C4SO: Diocese of Churches for the Sake of Others, a diocese of the Anglican Church in North America.
65 Brueggemann, *Awed to Heaven, Rooted in Earth*, 111. None of Brueggemann's prayers have an Address.
66 Charles Hefling, in Hefling and Shattuck, *Oxford Guide to the Book of Common Prayer*, 3.
67 Trinitarian theology has become a central focus in much theology today. A good starting place is Roger E. Olson and Christopher A. Hall, *The Trinity*, Guides to Theology (Grand Rapids, MI: Wm. B. Eerdmans, 2002). The details of the early Christian controversy can be read in Lewis Ayres, *Nicaea and Its Legacy: An Approach to Fourth-Century Theology* (New York: Oxford

University Press, 2004). Had some theologians learned the simple lesson that one does not move from humans to God and that neither does one ground marital relations in the Godhead, the theological disaster of eternal subordination of the Son would have been avoided. For robust defenses of orthodox Trinitarian thinking among evangelicals, see now Fred Sanders and Scott R. Swain, eds., *Retrieving Eternal Generation* (Grand Rapids, MI: Zondervan, 2017); Michael F. Bird and Scott Harrower, eds., *Trinity Without Hierarchy: Reclaiming Nicene Orthodoxy in Evangelical Theology* (Grand Rapids, MI: Kregel Academic, 2019).

68 Morley, *All Desires Known.*

69 Again, I have limited the Collects for this study mostly to the Sunday Collects. In the *Book of Common Prayer* there are approximately sixty more for more specific occasions, including days on which we remember saints like St. Stephen, St. Peter, and St. Paul. Including these would intensify the numbers but not change them in balance.

70 One cannot begin at a better location than a long stop with J. I. Packer, *Knowing God*, 20th Anniversary ed. (Downers Grove, IL: IVP, 1993).

71 Roger E. Olson, *Arminian Theology: Myths and Realties* (Downers Grove, IL: IVP Academic, 2006), 115–36.

72 John Goldingay, *Biblical Theology: The God of the Christian Scriptures* (Downers Grove, IL: IVP Academic, 2016), 42–43, 48.

73 Both Canaanite and Greek religions thought of God as father who (physically, literally) bore children, and this could explain the Old Testament's reticence. See Goldingay, *Biblical Theology* 37–38.

74 Scot McKnight, *A New Vision for Israel: The Teachings of Jesus in National Context* (Grand Rapids, MI: Wm. B. Eerdmans, 1999), 49–65.

75 Stephens-Hodge, *The Collects*, 17.

76 See also Hebrews 13:21; 1 Peter 4:11; Jude 25.

77 Goldingay, *The First Testament*, 923.

78 Stephens-Hodge, *The Collects*, 19.

79 Nichols, *The Collect.*

80 In the Reformed Churches this Collect is the prayer of illumination, and offered by the preacher, and is more focused on the Scripture texts to be read and then expounded. See Paul Galbreath, "Between Form and Freedom: The History of the Collect in the Reformed Tradition," in Nichols, *The Collect,* 123–38.

81 For a wise and wider approach, see David A. deSilva, *Sacramental Life: Spiritual Formation Through the Book of Common Prayer* (Downers Grove, IL: IVP Books, 2008).

82 Vanhoozer, *The Drama of Doctrine*, 32–33.

83 Hefling and Shattuck, *Oxford Guide to BCP*, 1.

84 Lauren F. Winner, *The Dangers of Christian Practice: On Wayward Gifts, Characteristic Damage, and Sin* (New Haven, CT: Yale University Press, 2018), 16.

85 Winner, *The Dangers of Christian Practice,* 79.

86 Winner, *The Dangers of Christian Practice,* 84.

87 William Zinsser, *On Writing Well: The Classic Guide to Writing Nonfiction*, 30th Anniversary ed. (New York: Harper Perennial, 2016), 6–16.

88 Stephens-Hodge, *The Collects*, 19.

89 In his foreword to Hefling and Shattuck, *Oxford Guide to BCP*, xiii.

ABOUT PARACLETE PRESS

WHO WE ARE

As the publishing arm of the Community of Jesus, Paraclete Press presents a full expression of Christian belief and practice—from Catholic to Evangelical, from Protestant to Orthodox, reflecting the ecumenical charism of the Community and its dedication to sacred music, the fine arts, and the written word. We publish books, recordings, sheet music, and video/DVDs that nourish the vibrant life of the church and its people.

WHAT WE ARE DOING

BOOKS | PARACLETE PRESS BOOKS show the richness and depth of what it means to be Christian. While Benedictine spirituality is at the heart of who we are and all that we do, our books reflect the Christian experience across many cultures, time periods, and houses of worship.

We have many series, including *Paraclete Essentials*; *Paraclete Fiction*; *Paraclete Poetry*; *Paraclete Giants*; and for children and adults, *All God's Creatures*, books about animals and faith; and *San Damiano Books*, focusing on Franciscan spirituality. Others include *Voices from the Monastery* (men and women monastics writing about living a spiritual life today), *Active Prayer*, and new for young readers: *The Pope's Cat*. We also specialize in gift books for children on the occasions of Baptism and First Communion, as well as other important times in a child's life, and books that bring creativity and liveliness to any adult spiritual life.

The MOUNT TABOR BOOKS series focuses on the arts and literature as well as liturgical worship and spirituality; it was created in conjunction with the Mount Tabor Ecumenical Centre for Art and Spirituality in Barga, Italy.

MUSIC | PARACLETE PRESS DISTRIBUTES RECORDINGS of the internationally acclaimed choir *Gloriæ Dei Cantores*, the *Gloriæ Dei Cantores Schola*, and the other instrumental artists of the *Arts Empowering Life Foundation*.

PARACLETE PRESS IS THE EXCLUSIVE NORTH AMERICAN DISTRIBUTOR for the Gregorian chant recordings from St. Peter's Abbey in Solesmes, France. Paraclete also carries all of the Solesmes chant publications for Mass and the Divine Office, as well as their academic research publications.

In addition, PARACLETE PRESS SHEET MUSIC publishes the work of today's finest composers of sacred choral music, annually reviewing over 1,000 works and releasing between 40 and 60 works for both choir and organ.

VIDEO | Our video/DVDs offer spiritual help, healing, and biblical guidance for a broad range of life issues including grief and loss, marriage, forgiveness, facing death, understanding suicide, bullying, addictions, Alzheimer's, and Christian formation.

Learn more about us at our website:
www.paracletepress.com
or phone us toll-free at 1.800.451.5006

SCAN
TO
READ

YOU MAY ALSO BE INTERESTED IN THESE TITLES BY
SCOT MCKNIGHT...

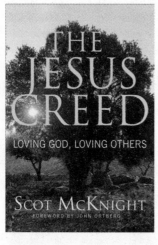

The Jesus Creed
Loving God, Loving Others
Foreword by John Ortberg

ISBN 978-1-61261-578-3
Trade paperback | $16.99

A remarkable summary of what biblical
Christianity is at its core. McKnight
fosters a practical understanding,
appreciation of, and application of
Christian formation in grace and love
toward God and Neighbor.

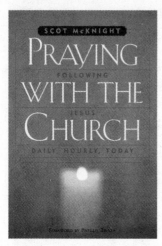

Praying with the Church
Following Jesus Daily, Hourly, Today
Foreword by Phyllis Tickle

ISBN 978-1-55725-481-8
Trade paperback | $18.95

McKnight invites all Christians who
desire to know more about the devotional
traditions of the Christian faith to get
closer to the heart of Jesus' message, by
discovering the ancient rhythms of daily
prayer at the heart of the early church.

Available at bookstores
Paraclete Press | 1-800-451-5006
www.paracletepress.com